LIGHTNING
NEVER STRIKES TWICE
(IF YOU OWN A FEATHER BED)

LIGHTNING
NEVER STRIKES TWICE
(IF YOU OWN A FEATHER BED)

and 1904 Other
American Superstitions
from the Ordinary to the Eccentric

VERGILIUS FERM

GRAMERCY PUBLISHING COMPANY
New York

Originally published as *A Brief Dictionary of American Superstitions*

Copyright © 1987, 1959 by The Philosophical Library, Inc.
All rights reserved.

This 1989 edition is published by Gramercy Publishing Company,
distributed by Crown Publishers, Inc.,
225 Park Avenue South, New York, New York 10003,
by arrangement with Philosophical Library.

Printed and Bound in the United States of America

Library of Congress Cataloging-in-Publication Data

Ferm, Vergilius Ture Anselm, 1896-1974.
    [Brief dictionary of American superstitions]
    Lightning never strikes twice (if you own a feather bed) : and
  1904 other American superstitions from the ordinary to the eccentric
    Vergilius Ferm.
        p.   cm.
    Rev. ed. of: A brief dictionary of American superstitions. 1959.
    1. Superstition—United States—Dictionaries.   I. Ferm, Vergilius
  Ture Anselm, 1896-1974. Brief dictionary of American superstitions.
  II. Title.
  BF1775.F47   1989
  001.9′6′0973—dc19   88-32724
                                                           CIP

ISBN 0-517-68025-4
h g f e d c b a

To My Grandchildren

DANNY

BILLY

DAVEY

LIN

JUDY

BOBBY

SUZY

ERIC

INTRODUCTION

In the multiplicity and variety of superstitions there is no end. Involving as they do men's utter credulity and emotional bias they touch upon every human interest; no one appears immune to his fair portion in the limitless collection. Superstitions are not confined to people whom we like to call "naive and gullible" but pervade the thought-life and activities of the wise, the discriminating and even the formally educated.

This book is not an encyclopedia but rather an organized sampling from the vast storehouse of the subject, a modest hand-book of a fractional portion of a vast literature. The author feels that he has finished his task with the cruel sense that he has but commenced it—ringing down the curtain while the play is still going strong.

A superstition generally bears no water-mark of its source. In this it is like people who generally have no clear knowledge of their parentage beyond a few generations. A superstition crosses oceans with emigrations and becomes mingled and mixed with indigenous notions. It defies the full light of reason since it is rooted in the deeper centers of motivation— in feelings, habits, prejudices, desires, fears, hopes and in uncritical social customs. In its core it is endowed with a power which sweeps away criticism. The scientific mind is its worst enemy; but the scientific mind is the result of persistent discipline to which human nature is not easily given—particularly in all areas. A superstition like a weed grows on the finest lawns of better knowledge, persisting alongside the most cultivated areas of the mind. There is probably no one without his clusters of them. When some crisis comes into our lives we readily recall some relevant superstition and summon it to our aid.

One does not need to know the origin of a thing to respect it. A superstition is as powerful without proper portfolio as with one. It needs no blue-blood parentage nor even the suggestion of any relatives. Generally, it is an orphan abandoned long ago by parents at some door-step where it has been picked up anonymously. Scholars may trace its ancestors but it performs and persists on its own.

A superstition may sound silly. But silly it never intended to be. It is a serious artifact of the mind bearing the promise of success, failure, hope or despair to those who embrace it. Many superstitions unwittingly bear in them elements of truth without passing muster before the critical criteria of truth. Their truths, if any, are disguised by false references. Remedies, for example, which grandmother summoned for family illnesses may sometime have worked pragmatically although linked to seemingly incredible concepts. Whatever we may think about a superstition it stands as a fact to itself and is a fact in any account of the history of folklore.

Definitions of superstitions have been suggested without number. Webster's Dictionary account of it is to characterize it as "an irrational . . . attitude of mind . . . proceeding from ignorance." The Oxford Dictionary account of it describes it as "an unreasoning awe or fear of something unknown or mysterious, especially in connection with religion, religious belief founded on fear or ignorance."

William Lyon Phelps, Yale's once celebrated literary critic, offered this comment: "The best definition of superstition that I can remember was made by James Russell Lowell: 'Superstition, by which I mean the respecting of that which we are told to respect rather than that which is respectable in itself' " and added one of his own: "superstition is a form of slavery, because the mind is subjected to fear. As notoriety is the bastard sister of reputation so superstition is the bastard sister of religion."

To a long list of definitions this Introduction may offer another: "A superstition is any belief or practice whose trusted efficacy is independent of and contrary to the foundations of critical truth and objective fact." This efficacy feeds upon a non-logical or illogical temper of mind and upon conservative temperaments operating in certain areas of interest; it demands no coherence in a critical system of ideas, often committing common fallacies of thought (e.g., the fallacy of *post hoc ergo propter hoc*, which means that a succession of two events is taken as a *necessary* relation of cause-effect); it nourishes itself upon the indiscriminate practice of hypostasizing human experiences into things or forces (e.g., a satisfied experience is translated into a thing called "Luck"); it enjoys the exhilaration of a quick solution of a problem that is not otherwise readily resolved or even faced, the exhilaration of positive certainty and assurance which is a prize possession of impatient and restless spirits; and it entrenches itself in a security that comes with an emotional commitment not easily eradicated by critical examination.

In this book there are systematic recordings of some of the more-or-less common American superstitions as data of human interest, without any attempt to explain them, evaluate their claims or trace their complicated origins. American superstitions—except Indian—are far from purely native; they are American in practice and setting but belong, on the whole, to the gathering folk lore of the not too distant immigrations from other lands. Materials change but forms of the long yesterdays persist.

A superstition has one characteristic that makes it stand out in folk lore: linked with a profound emotion it can play havoc with a life. It can weigh a person down with the most fearful of fears and chain his every act into a fitful self-consciousness. It can make a fool of a person more easily than any jesting and it can nurture idiosyncracies into intolerable manners of behavior. In a world so uncertain as ours, with possibilities so complex, superstitions will continue to flourish among minds sensitive to the hazards of everyday living. If there is but a grain of chance that some superstition will bring about a benediction in a frustrating situation man will grasp it as a drowning person grasps for a twig.

This is a casual book for casual use. It is the product of a casual avocation on the part of its author whose literary work has followed the path of more serious themes in the fields of philosophy, theology and religion. It must be frankly confessed that a large void is to be noticed in this Dictionary: the area of superstitions found in *religious* ideas and practices of Americans. To fill such a void would be to tread upon sensitive toes and to stir up a vicious anathema upon the work and even a hex upon its author. But it is undoubtedly true that the best religions of our times promulgate superstitions of a long heritage which only the perspective of time will recognize as such and thus form data for a more complete companionable volume.

Vergilius Ferm

LIGHTNING

NEVER STRIKES TWICE

(IF YOU OWN A FEATHER BED)

A

abracadabra:
See words.

absence makes the heart grow fonder:
Temporary absence between people may sustain the slogan; but protracted absence between them tends to refute it. The superstition is involved in making a slogan into a law of life which it is not intended to be.

absent-minded professors:
See memory.

accident prevention:
See baby shoes.

accidents:
Accidents are believed by some to come in threes. See dressing.

aches:
See cures; pain.

acorns:
Carry an acorn and you will have good luck, especially a long life. An acorn is a charm. See dreams.

acrophobia:
See phobias.

actors and actresses:
See black; catchword; Cowl, Jane; Craven, Frank; cross-eyed people; Cumberland, John; Eagels, Jeanne; Jolson, Al; Macbeth; make-up box; peacock; Rogers, Will; theatre; Vaughan, Sarah; whistling back stage; yellow.

Adams, Evangeline:
See astrology.

adult learning:
See learning.

advertisements:
See athletes.

affection:
See colors.

age levels:
See learning.

aggressiveness:
See chin and jaw.

agoraphobia:
See phobias.

agriculture:
See moon, the new.

air plane:
See Washington, Dinah.

Alexandrite:
See wedding anniversaries.

almond:
An almond in rice pudding drawn by a guest's spoon will bring good luck. (A Swedish-American superstition.) Marriage is in the offing for the lucky eligible one.

aluminum:
See wedding anniversaries.

aluminum cooking utensils:
There was a widespread rumor and belief that food in contact with aluminum turned to poison. (Discredited by the

United States Public Health Service and the American Medical Association [*Nature*, March 25, 1933]).

ambition:
See palmistry.

American Indians:
See birds; four; mounds; preaching to the fish; Pueblo tribes; wands, magic; St. Germain.

amethyst:
See birth stones; wedding anniversaries.

Amish:
See fences; hooks and eyes; ministers and bishops; moon, the; musical instruments.

amulets:
An amulet is anything carried or worn to protect the person from misfortune or bring good luck. A pebble may serve, a four-leaf clover, gold beetle, a coin, spectacles, old shoes, a rosary, medal, etc. Many American celebrities have admitted this practice. For example, Carole Lombard, the actress, is said to have carried a smooth round pebble (gift of Clark Gable); Pat O'Brien, the actor, is said to carry a four-leaf clover; Cecil B. de Mille, the cinema producer, is said to wear a uniform of riding breeches for work; Bette Davis, the actress, is said to carry a gold beetle; George Brent, the actor, is said to prefer an old Irish shilling.

There is no limit to these possibilities. See charm, lucky; luck, bad; luck, good; talisman; words.

angel, vision of:
See praying mantis.

anger:
See colors.

animal grease:
See cures.

3

animal magnetism:
See metallic tractors; mesmerism.

animals:
See Davy Crockett; evil eye; fortune telling; mounds; scapulimancy.

anniversaries, wedding:
See wedding anniversaries.

announcing a project beforehand:
It is considered to invite bad luck to announce beforehand a project not yet completed. An author, for example, may feel it hazardous to announce a work which has not yet reached the printing stage. To do so he may feel to be too great a risk of disappointment. See incompletion.

Anti-Superstition Society:
As recently as Friday, June 13th, 1958, "one hundred stalwart men and their guests"—according to the *Chicago Daily Tribune* (issue of June 14th, 1958) met in the Chicago Athletic Club bravely to defy the hoax of superstitions particularly associated with Friday, the 13th. Under the reported leadership of Ben Regan, the Anti-Superstition Society composed of "aldermen, judges, and leaders of the business and industrial community," with 13 vice-presidents, defied the bad luck spells associated with broken mirrors, black cats, ladders, opened umbrellas, etc. Greetings posted on the walls read "Mississippi Black Cat Society," "Salem Witchcraft, Inc.," etc.

Some dozen years earlier the company met in a mortuary and sat around an open coffin upon which stood 13 candles.

Guests of honor included such names as Ward Quaal, vice president and general manager of W-G-N, Inc., George Halas, coach and owner of the Chicago Bears. Quaal was reported to have been presented a gold wrist-watch with all the numerals on the dial marked "13."

The purpose of the organization aside from its social

4

interest is to evidence a disregard for the superstitions of Friday, the 13th.

ants:

See dreams; ridding a house of ants; weather prognostication.

appendicitis:

See grape seeds.

apple:

We are all familiar with the old saying: "An apple a day keeps the doctor away." This saying carries some grains of truth in that a much needed mineral (potassium) is found in an apple.

apple love divination:

In New England an apple's division was performed to determine the love-fate of a person. The number of seeds determined the fate:

One, I love
Two, I love
Three, I love, I say
Four, I love with all my heart
And five, I cast away;
Six, he loves
Seven, she loves
Eight, they both love;
Nine, he comes
Ten, he tarries
Eleven, he courts
Twelve, he marries;
Thirteen, wishes
Fourteen, kisses
All the rest little witches.

See peeling of an apple.

apple peeling:
See cures; peeling an apple.

apple-root, bitter:
See voodoo.

Appleseed, Johnny:
See Johnny Appleseed.

apple trees:
See Christmas prognostication.

April:
See birth stones; marriage.

April Fool's Day:
The day of practical jokes. A world-wide day of celebration: the first of April. Celebrated by ancients as the beginning of the vernal equinox amidst general frolicking.

To be fooled by a pretty maiden signifies that you will marry her or befriend her (if she is single).

To lose one's temper at a practical joke on April Fool's Day will bring bad luck.

If a wedding occurs on April Fool's Day this signifies that the woman will be "the boss" in the family. If one's birthday occurs on this day one will be lucky in business and unlucky in speculation.

April showers:
Widely quoted prediction:

> April showers
> Bring May flowers.

April 30:
See witches.

apron dropping:
It is an omen of something impending, inadvertently to drop an apron. It may be the meeting of the girl's fiancé; it

6

may signify the marriage to two husbands; it may signify illness or early death; it may mean many children, no children or even spinsterhood; it may mean desertion by a husband. Europeans have many interpretations.

aquamarine:
See birth stones.

Aquarius:
See astrology; birth stones.

Aries:
See astrology; birth stones.

arms:
See hair; starting on a journey.

arson:
See moon, the new.

artistic character:
See palmistry.

ass:
See weather prognostication.

asthma:
See cures.

astrology:
The "science" of signs or omens based on the stars. Superstitions are as old (and older) as man's interest in the heavenly bodies. Astrology was practiced as a great art by the Chaldeans and found in the theories of ancient religions. Even the Star of Bethlehem is an ancient remnant of an ancient astrological superstition.

To this day, in America, astrology is extremely and widely popular. Many periodicals issue from the presses and many articles appear in newspapers devoted to the art of astrology. Evangeline Adams, a popular astrologer, numbered among her clients such patrons as J. Pierpont Morgan, Mary Garden and many other famous people. Warren G. Harding (president of the United States) and his wife are said to have consulted the astrologer Marcia.

Children still repeat the old rhyme:

Star light, star bright
First star I've seen tonight;
I wish I may, I wish I might
Have the wish I wish tonight.

A falling star is a sign of bad luck or death. However, if one says "money, money, money" before its disappearance, good luck will come—in the form of money.

The moon is the traditional focus of attention for superstitious agriculturalists. (See moon.)

The Zodiac is the center of "astrological science." This is the path through which planets were observed to travel. The signs of the Zodiac reveal fate and fortune. "Fixed stars" were combined into "constellations" or groups and their patterns were given names taken from mythological lore. Constellation patterns marked the changing seasons. The affairs of men were taken to depend upon the changing patterns of the sky. The heavens declare men's fortunes—if only the patterns can be properly read. Astrology is the "science" of reading these patterns and foretelling the future.

Each constellation has its significance. Aries, the Ram, dominant from March 21 to April 20 is the constellation of certain promise. If one is born under this pattern one will be an energetic person, full of courage, short in tact, impatient and intolerant. (This is the constellation of Walter Winchell, Charlie Chaplin!)

Taurus, the Bull, dominant from April 21 to May 22. If one is born under this pattern one will be practical, good-natured, placid, artistic, patient and dignified. Only in anger do such people show stubbornness. (This is the constellation of Adolf Hitler, Karl Marx, Shirley Temple, Bishop Manning!) Gemini, the Twins, dominant from May 23 to June 21. If one is born under this pattern one will be witty, carefree, charming, lively, breezy and even humorous. (This is the constellation of Jimmy Walker, James A. Farley, Al Jolson!)

Cancer, the Crab, dominant from June 22 to July 22. If one is born under this pattern one, like the crab, will be tenacious, meditative, worrisome. (This is the constellation of Calvin Coolidge, Jack Dempsey, Irvin Cobb, Ely Culbertson!)

Leo, the Lion, dominant from July 23 to August 22. If one is born under this pattern one will be ambitious, magnanimous, proud, staunch, dictatorial. (This is the constellation of Herbert Hoover, Harry Lauder, Bruce Barton!) Virgo, the Virgin, dominant from August 23 to September 23. If one is born under this pattern one will be intellectual, cool, efficient, conscientious, hypocritical. (This is the constellation of Greta Garbo, Savonarola, St. Augustine!)

Libra, the Balance, dominant from September 24 to October 21. If one is born under this pattern one will be charming, gracious, harmonious, noble and peaceful. (This is the constellation of Eugene O'Neill, Cordell Hull, Christopher Columbus!) Scorpio, the Scorpion, dominant from October 22 to November 21. If one is born under this pattern one will be shrewd, intense, industrious, substantial. (This is the constellation of Booker T. Washington, Paderewski, Daniel Boone!)

Sagittarius, the Archer, dominant from November 22 to December 21. If one is born under this pattern one will be friendly, optimistic, brilliant, healthy and generous. (This is the constellation of Winston Churchill, John Bunyan!) Capricorn, the Goat, dominant from December 21 to January 21. If one is born under this pattern one will be serious, methodical, ambitious, dignified, honorable. (This is the constellation of Paul Revere, Carl Sandburg!)

Aquarius, the Water Bearer, dominant from January 22 to February 19. If one is born under this pattern one will be high strung, erratic, brilliant, unpredictable. (This is the con-

9

stellation of Franklin D. Roosevelt, Abraham Lincoln, Thomas Edison!) Pisces, dominant from February 20 to March 20. If one is born under this pattern one will be gentle, tender, sympathetic, soft and dreamy. (This is the constellation of George Washington, Andrew Jackson!)

Planets are associated with character traits: the moon with melancholy, romance and femininity; Mercury, with intellect, mental ability, alertness; Saturn, with caution, seriousness, thrift; Jupiter, with honor and joviality; Mars, with courage and power; and Venus, with love and refinement.

Numbers play an important part in astrology. One's name, e.g., can by its numerical value foretell the future. The heavens declare the importance of number and thus suggest dates. See birth stones.

athletes:

Many superstitions persist among athletic competitors.

Among baseball players, it is a sign of good luck to see a load of empty barrels. A ball player will doff his cap upon seeing such a sight. Good luck is attracted by the rubbing of the head of a Negro bell-hop. To prevent bad luck, a ball player will spit in his hat at the sight of a cross-eyed woman.

There are pet individual superstitions among ball players. Eddie Collins, manager of the Chicago White Sox, wore a lucky undershirt in all championship games although it was worn almost to shreds. He stuck a piece of chewing gum to the button of his cap which he removed to chew only when he had two strikes against him.

Pitchers have their superstitions. Some baseball pitchers insist that, for good luck, their glove be left palm down near the mound; some keep the glove in the hip pocket when out of the pitching box. Following an identical course to the bench brings good luck to some ball players. Others will studiously avoid walking between the catcher and the umpire. Some avoid stepping on chalk lines or step over with the left foot first.

George Stallings, former manager of the Boston Braves, forbade yellow advertisements in the ball park and yellow worn by his team. Upon a rally, he remained fixed (even uncomfortably) in his position as long as the rally continued. He regarded pigeons, papers or peanut shells in front of his bench as harboring bad luck.

It is bad luck to play with a bat split even though a minor one; to have any part of a player's uniform missing or torn. A mascot can bring good or bad luck and persistent wins or losses may be charged to him.

It is good luck to a ball player to touch second base. (One famous center-fielder insisted on stepping on second base each time he went on and off the playing field.) It is bad luck for the team whose first man at plate fans out.

Among old-time ball players it was considered good luck to spit in their gloves (an act of magic?).

A bat should never be changed after strike two.

Bats should never be left lying crosswise.

A broken bat is a sign of a batting slump.

A dog crossing the playing field before the first pitch will bring bad luck.

A "south-paw" pitcher (left-handed) is usually considered a good luck charm. The team which loses the first innings will win at the end.

Golfers have their pet superstitions. Edward Ray, British champion, stuck his black pipe in his mouth for good luck. Some golfers approach the tee from the rear; others take sand from the tee-box and sprinkle the ground. Glenna Collett walked on the same side of the bunker as her caddie; when a match was going successfully she would not clean the golf ball.

There are, of course, many superstitions associated with other sports and athletic contests. See prize fighters.

atomic bomb tests:
The birth of what may well be a superstition is the con-

11

clusion drawn from the atomic bomb tests: that such explosions are responsible for tornadoes, hurricanes, floods, bad weather, etc. Scientists point out the fact that tornadoes and hurricanes, etc., have been occurring for a long, long time and even frequently, before such tests.

August:
See birth stones; marriage.

August 1:
See witches.

author:
See announcing a project beforehand.

authority:
See wand, magic.

automobile:
See car washing.

autumn:
See weather prognostication.

B

baby:
See beads and teeth; birth with a veil; biting nails; children; cross-eyed people; Good Friday; grow up hideous; hair; hypnotism; lice; nail cutting; sneezing; tickling babies; witches.

baby shoes:
A pair of miniature baby shoes hung on the inside of the cab of a truck is held to protect the driver against accident.

bachelor:
A bachelor is said to be "jolly." A slogan superstitious in implication. It is quite unfounded. (Is the bachelor really "jolly" or is this description that of envy on the part of disillusioned married men? Statistics show that the odds are against a bachelor's felicity: his suicide rate is higher [as a class]; he belongs among those with a higher rate of mental disturbances; he is more susceptible to disease; [*Why Are You Single?*, edited by H. Holland, 1949, pp. 78-81]).
See bachelorhood; spinster.

bachelorhood:
See bachelor; bread; mirror.

back ache:
See cures.

backwards:
See cow; Devil, the.

bacon:
See moon.

bad disposition:
See cross (disposition).

bad fortune:
See onomancy.

bad luck:
See luck, bad.

bad news:
See birds; ear burning or ringing; rooster.

bad omens:
See omens, bad.

bad spirits:
See evil spirits.

bad temper:
See April Fool's Day; card playing; meat eating.

bad weather:
See moon; weather prognostication.

baggage:
See valise; yellow.

Bainter, Fay:
See yellow.

bait:
See spitting.

baking:
The first cake taken from the oven should not be cut but broken; otherwise, all subsequent cakes baked on the same day will be soggy.

Among the North Carolina legends baking a cake while menstruating will cause it to turn out ill. Cake baking should occur while the sun is going up. It is bad luck to throw away eggshells until after the cake is baked. It is bad luck to walk

14

across the floor while the cake is baking. It is good luck to stop the clock during the process.

See clockwise.

bald eagle:
See birds.

baldness:
If a bald-headed man washes his head with sage tea this will bring out a new crop of hair (New England).

See cures; flies; memory; rum.

Ballard, G. W.:
See spiritual vibrations; St. Germain.

balsam fir:
See cures.

banana stalks:
A banana stalk hung in the chicken house will rid the place of chicken lice (Ozarks). Occasionally a banana stalk may be seen hanging in an out-building.

bananas:
Eating bananas will make a person fat.

banquet:
See empty seat.

baptism of a child:
See children.

bark:
See pine bark.

barns:
See May; moon, the; red.

barrels, empty:
See athletes.

15

bar-tenders:
See glassware.

baseball:
See athletes.

bath:
See salesmen; singing.

bats:
See birds; weather prognostication.

Baun, Florence:
See theatre.

beads and teeth:
A rather prevalent superstition held by American mothers of a couple of generations ago was to the effect that the hanging of amber beads around a newborn baby's neck assured it of less irritation of the gums in teething and result in a good set of teeth. Sometimes tiny grayish seeds (Job's tears) were substituted for the beads.

bear brains:
See cures.

bear skins:
See cures.

beau:
See fortune telling.

beauty:
See fortune telling.

beauty patch:
See mole or wart.

beaver's fat:
See cures.

Beazely, Almira:
See rappings.

bed:

See cramps; getting out of bed; hat on bed; hat under bed; jumping out of bed; strange bed; thunderstorm; turning over in bed; hops in a pillow.

bed bugs:

Bed bugs have been associated with many cures. As an ointment for sore eyes, crushed bed bugs mixed with salt and human milk afford relief. Taken internally in powder form bed bugs will cure a fever and relieve hysteria. In certain areas of Ohio a mixture of bed bugs and beans was believed to cure chills and fever. As an antidote to poisons bed bugs have been considered useful.

See birds.

bed making:

See three.

beef, fresh:

See dreams.

beer:

See cures; glassware.

bees:

A common belief in New England (and in the Ozarks) was to the effect that bees must be made aware of the death of a member of the family, otherwise they would desert the hive or leave their tasks and themselves die. To acquaint them the housewife hung upon the stand of hives something black—the symbol of mourning—usually humming to herself some doleful tune; sometimes the master of the house would tap upon the hives, saying quietly that so-and-so had died. Whittier refers to this superstitious custom in one of his "Home Ballads."

Southern Negroes are highly superstitious when it comes to bees. For example, bees seen in swarms foretell death; a bee sting means a betrayal; a dream about bees making honey

17

is a sign of honor; a dream about killing a bee suggests some forthcoming loss.

It is risky to sell a beehive without further ritual. A bee sale should be accompanied with another corresponding transaction of value (such as a bushel of corn). The following saying suggests changing values of bees:

A swarm of bees in May
Is worth a load of hay.
A swarm of bees in June
Is worth a silver spoon.
A swarm of bees in July
Is not worth a fly!

It is a western Pennsylvania saying that bees single out red-headed persons, overlook idiots and people with good dispositions.

A yellow honey bee flying around a person is a sign of forthcoming good news (Louisiana); if it is black, beware of bad news.

It is a common belief that a bee ignored will not sting. (Unfortunately, not true!)

A bee flying into a window is the omen of good news.

A bee stings but once. (Unfortunately, this is not always true!)

Beating pans, ringing cowbells or making noise generally, is supposed to scare swarming bees and induce them to settle down. (It is doubtful that bees hear sounds.)

Before cutting down a tree with bees in it (to obtain honey) say certain magic words (e.g., begin with "ema ema") and you will not suffer stinging. (Pennsylvania)

See sailors; weather prognostication.

beetles:
See horsemen; weather prognostication.

18

beetles (wood boring):
A beetle heard tapping in the wall of a house is a warning of death.
See ear ache; horsemen.

beet sugar:
See cane sugar.

beggar:
It is a sign of bad luck to meet a beggar soon after leaving one's house in the morning. One must return and begin again.

beginning something:
See Saturday.

behind the eight ball:
See eight.

bell hop, Negro:
See athletes.

benevolence:
See phrenology.

beryl:
See birth stones.

betrayal:
See bees.

betrothal:
See engagement for marriage.

betting:
See money.

Bible carrying:
See carrying a holy book.

Bible divination:
A common practice for the credulous in divination is to

open the Bible and place the index finger at random on the text. The message, in case of distress, will suggest the solution. If the words have no bearing to the particular distress the message is unfavorable.

To ask a question on a doubtful matter open the Bible and note the first word on the left-hand page. If the word has letters adding up to an even number the answer is "No"; if the addition gives an odd number the answer is "Yes."

When discouraged, open the Bible and repeat:

Mark and Matthew, Luke and John
Counsel, that I may get on.

Inspiration will follow during your sleep.

An old English custom is the laying of the Bible on the table on New Year's Day, each member of the household opening at random and reading the prediction of things to come for the New Year from suggested contents of the two open pages.

The Book of Proverbs contains in its last chapter (31) thirty one verses. Each signifies references to a day of the month. Consulting the verse corresponding to the day of the month of one's birth will indicate the most successful occupation or vocation for the consultant. Verse twenty-four tells of "fine linen": an indication of a successful career as merchant or relevant area.

There is no end to possibilities in divination in consulting a book regarded as holy.

See ministers and bishops.

bibliomancy:
The art of reading into the future by consulting some book, sacred or secular.

big feet:
A sign of intelligence.

big toe:
    See fish-bone.

bird feathers:
    See feathers.

bird of wisdom:
    See birds.

birds:

Birds have symbolized spirits. Associated with both good and bad spirits. The dove, for example, is the symbol of the Holy Spirit (often found suspended over a pulpit where the Word of God's Spirit is believed to be proclaimed).

Birds are portents of things to come. A bird's appearance within a house is an omen of death. (Interior decorators are aware of this superstition in their encounter with people who avoid using wall paper with bird designs.) A bird tapping on a window is also an omen of death (spirit calling to spirit).

Ornithomancy is the term for the art and practice of divining events from the behavior of birds.

A robin is an omen of both good and bad luck. It should not be injured nor its nest disturbed—if good luck is to come. A friendly robin is a portent of a long and hard winter. In the spring the first robin encountered will bring good luck if it flies up, bad luck if it flies down. A robin's nest near one's house is an omen of good luck. A robin appearing in the morning is the sign of a visitor coming on the same day. A robin held prisoner in the house brings bad luck.

If the robin sings in the bush
The weather will be coarse;
If the robin sings on the barn
The weather will be warm.

If a swallow abandons its nest on a house this is a sign of the burning down of the house. A nest under the eaves of a house brings good luck to its inhabitants. Swallows skimming close to the ground (feeding on insects) suggest rain.

Famous in America is the coming of the swallows to the Mission San Juan Capistrano (near San Diego, California). Their coming is predicted for St. Joseph's Day, March 19; their going, for San Juan's Day, October 23. These swallows are alleged to come and go with regularity on these days since the mission's founding some 150 years ago. The sacred tradition was broken in the fall of 1940, upsetting the annual festivities of the mission fathers.

Swallows are good-luck birds. It is unlucky to kill a swallow. When in the spring a swallow is heard to sing one goes to a fountain or stream, washes his eyes, says a prayer, and the swallow carries away troubles associated with the eyes.

When the swallow's nest is high,
Summer is dry;
When the swallow's nest is low,
You can safely reap and sow.

Swift-flying "chimney swifts" nestling in a chimney are said to attract bed-bugs to a house. A legend concerns their return to and departure from San Juan Capistrano, timed with the appearance and disappearance of the swallows, taking immediate possession of the nests vacated by the swallows.

Canaries are subjects of superstitions. A strange cat which kills a pet canary means bad luck for two years. A dead canary is a sign to him who comes upon it that blood will be shed the same day. A strange canary flying into a house spells death to a member of the family. Pet canaries (along with dogs, gold fish and cats) are believed to bring harmony to a home.

If a sparrow builds a nest above one's window one may expect to be taking a trip.

Feeding strange pigeons will bring good luck. Pigeons

flying in a circle over a body of water prophesy rain. Pigeons which nest on the roof will bring good luck to the occupants of a house. The cooing of a turtle dove at a window indicates sad news. Turtle doves near a house will dispel rheumatism. A change in weather will be certain when doves are unusually noisy.

The cuckoo's call on the first of May is a prognostication of the kind of season ahead. From the north the call suggests tragedy; from the south a good harvest; from the west, good luck; from the east happy romancing. The maiden kisses her hand and says to the cuckoo's May call:

> Cuckoo, cuckoo
> Tell me true
> When shall I be married?

The number it calls following this query signifies the number of years she must wait. Cuckoo superstitions abound in the southern states.

The stork bird is an omen of good luck, symbol of protection. A gobbling turkey is the speech of welcome. When a turkey stretches its neck, staring upwards, this is a sign of rain.

The breaking of a wish-bone of a chicken or turkey is a sign of good luck and fulfilled wish to the one who gets the long end of the break.

The cry of a peacock under a window signals the death of an occupant of the house.

> When the peacock loudly bawls,
> Soon you'll have both rain and squalls.

Theatrical people once shied away from wearing peacock feathers as harbingers of bad luck. The reverse is now true: they are good luck charms in the American theatre.

23

Bats are birds (actually mammals) of both good and bad omens. They are "witches" to some. To others they denote happiness, peace, long life, wealth and virtue.

Eagles (the "bald" [snow-white head] eagle, an American bird) are said to carry off lambs and children (an unfounded superstition).

The American Indians believed that an owl signals approaching death. As "the bird of wisdom" students carry owl charms to bring them good luck in examinations (e.g., Columbia University students).

A hawk is an omen of victory or success when seen flying overhead, in the act of decision or in a contest engaged by the observer. Sea hawks signify clear weather ahead. When flying low they predict rain and a rainbow. A hawk-skin is a lucky charm.

Crows are not so easily scared as the widespread belief in scare-crows indicates. A scare-crow (a disreputable looking representative of a man hung on a wooden cross) is probably the outgrowth of the idea of the protection of a cross against intruders and evil spirits. Part of the effectiveness of scare-crows is due to the odor of man which birds may scent.

Crow on the fence
Rain will go hence
Crow on the ground
Rain will come down.

A single crow cawing near a house is an omen of approaching calamity. A counter-charm is the removal of one's hat or a bow. The first crow seen in the spring in flight means that one will be taking a trip. A crow in flight to the left means bad news; if flying on the right this means to be on one's guard for the day. A crow in flight is the time to make a wish; if it continues in flight without flapping its wings the wish will come true; if it flaps its wings, one should look away if one's wish is to be fulfilled.

24

"As the crow flies" (a straight line) is a saying that is true only at the time of a crow's migration.

See black bird; chicken's wishbone; cledonism; crows; owl; peacock; pigeons; robin; sailors; weather prognostication.

birth:

A common superstition is to the effect that a child born in the summer will be brighter than if he were born at another season of the year. (An association with the power of the sun? Tests have failed to sustain the belief [*British Medical Journal*, March 4, 1944].)

If one is born during an eclipse this means that one will suffer poverty and misfortune.

See crows; prenatal influences; shooting stars and comets.

birthday:

See April Fool's Day; astrology; Christmas; February 29; fortune telling.

birthday candles:

See blowing out birthday candles.

birth mark:

A birth mark in the middle of the back is a sign of good luck and especially of future wealth.

See mole or wart; witches.

birth stones:

Stones have long been regarded as lucky charms. During the Middle Ages many ancient beliefs about stones were consummated into definite associations, particularly with the zodiac. Here is a 16th century arrangement by Cornelius Agrippa:

Aries (The Ram) April (the month in each case beginning about the 21st of the preceding month)—sardonyx

Taurus (The Bull) May—carnelian

Gemini (The Twins) June—topaz

Cancer (The Crab) July—chalcedony

Leo (The Lion) August—jasper
Virgo (The Virgin) September—emerald
Libra (The Balance) October—beryl
Scorpius (The Scorpion) November—amethyst
Sagittarius (The Archer) December—hyacinth (sapphire)
Capricornus (The Goat) January—chrysoprase
Aquarius (The Water bearer) February—crystal
Pisces (The Fishes) March—sapphire (lapis-lazuli)

The present use of birth stones has probably emerged from this custom of associating stones with the zodiac. An arbitrary list of "proper" stones for each month (lucky stones) was selected by the National Association of Retail Jewelers to guide its membership in advising the public. This selection is probably inspired by a Polish list of the 18th century (excepting the opal):

January—garnet (the birthstone in each case)
February—amethyst
March—bloodstone (or aquamarine)
April—diamond
May—emerald
June—pearl (or moonstone)
July—ruby
August—sardonyx
September—sapphire
October—opal (or tourmaline)
November—topaz (or topaz-quartz)
December—turquoise (or lapis-lazuli).
See astrology; stones.

birth with a veil:
Babies "born with a veil" are said to be especially gifted or favored.

This superstition does not take into consideration the physiological fact of a bit of membrane from the amniotic sac which occasionally covers a baby's face at birth.

bishops:
See ministers and bishops.

biting nails:
If a baby bites its nails it will develop stubby fingers.

black:
Black clothes worn on the stage is regarded by some actresses as foreboding real bereavement. Dark blue or green is usually substituted for a part that calls for black.

blackberries:
See dreams.

black bird:
If a black bird comes into a house this is a sign of death.
See birds.

black cards:
See card playing.

black cat:
If a black cat crosses one's path this is an omen of bad luck. However, a strange black cat making its home with one brings good luck.
See Devil, the; Friday, the 13th; theatre.

black dog:
See Devil, the.

black eye:
See meat eating.

blackeyed peas:
See pig-jowls.

black eyes:
See fortune telling.

black headed pin:
See pin.

black horse:
See horsemen.

black pig:
See Devil, the.

black stocking:
See cures.

black valise:
See sailors.

blankets:
Never wash blankets in a month that does not have an "r" in its name. To violate this principle is to invite bad luck.
See horsehair.

blankets, new:
See dreams.

bleeding:
See blood; nose bleeding; cures.

blessing:
See wand, magic.

Blessington, Lady:
See magic crystal.

blindness:
See flowers; moon.

blood:
See birds; bleeding; nose bleeding; racial superstition; sewing.

blood pressure:
See meat eating.

bloodstone:
See birth stones.

blowing a seedy dandelion:

Blow a seedy dandelion and count the remaining seeds. These will show the number of children you will have.

See dandelion.

blowing out birthday candles:

Successfully blowing out birthday candles (usually set on top of a birthday cake) in one breath, after making a wish, will make the wish come true. Such a birthday cake includes as many candles as the number of years of life already attained.

blue:

See star sapphire, blue; weather prognostication.

blue, dark:

See black.

blue eyes:

See fortune telling.

blue jays:

See weather prognostication.

blushing:

Blushing is a sign of lying.

boasting:

It is common among those working in the area of safety to avoid boasting of any improvement, such as a decrease in traffic accidents, building and bridge safety, etc. To say that an accident rate will drop is to invite trouble. Bragging about one's good fortune is to invite misfortune. To say "I haven't had a cold all winter" is to wake up the following day snuffling.

The magic phrase "touch wood" or the German "unberufen" or the Italian "scaramanzia" will soften the boast and avert disaster. A little rap of the knuckles on wood (or head!) will also help. Perhaps such practice will scare away the evil spirits.

See knock on wood.

boats:
See evil eye.

body contour:
See chin and jaw; physiognomy.

bogy man:
Children are taught to beware of the bogy man. He belongs to the class of goblins (evil spirits). Sometimes called "the bugaboo" or "the buggey," this spirit once was a supreme god now fallen to low estate, capable of doing harm to the innocent, lurking in dark corners, devil incarnate.

boiling water out of a kettle:
See storm.

boils:
Three nutmegs hung around the neck will cure boils (Maine).

A camphor bag hung around the neck will help get rid of boils (Maine).

bones:
See scapulimancy; storm.

book:
See author; carrying a holy book; examinations; wedding anniversaries.

Booker, Betty:
See fairy faith.

book reading:
See bibliomancy.

Bostic, Earl:
His good luck charm is to sing "Flamingo" as a warm-up before recording sessions.

bowing:
See moon, the new.

boy:
See crows.

Bradley, William:
See theatre.

bragging:
See boasting.

brain food:
See fish.

brandy, burnt:
See dog.

bread:
Taking the last piece of bread on a plate or to throw bread away is to invite bad luck.

To take the last piece of bread and butter on the table a bachelor may gain for himself a wife and money. An unmarried woman will remain unmarried if she takes it (or anything that is a last piece). Does this date back to the days when men seized women? Seizure of the last piece of bread and butter demonstrates man's supremacy in aggressiveness. A woman who boldly takes this initiative demonstrates a masculinity which scares off potential suitors.

Breaking bread into crumbs at the table is a sign of impending poverty.

Men who eat much bread will possess hairy chests.

See crust and crumbs; onions.

"bread and butter":
To say "bread and butter" is to break the spell of bad luck if someone or something passes between two people. Both people involved should say this phrase. See walking.

bread burning:
See burning bread.

31

bread carrying:
See bread crust; moving into a new home.

bread crumbs:
See crust and crumbs; hair.

bread crust:
It is good luck to carry a crust of bread in the pocket or pocketbook.
Eating bread crusts will make rosy cheeks.
See crust and crumbs.

bread falling:
If bread falls butter-side down, this is a sign that company is coming hungry for food.

breakfast, after:
See dreams.

breakfast, before:
See dreams; memory; sing before breakfast; sneezing.

breaking a dish:
See waiters at tables.

breaking a friendship:
See glove.

breaking a glass:
See bridegroom; mirrors; toasting.

breaking a hair:
See fortune telling.

breaking a mirror:
See mirror.

breaking bread:
See bread.

breaking friendships:
See friends.

breaking pottery:
See Good Friday.

bride:
Brides may scoff at the idea but many still practice the old slogan which, pointing to good luck, advises them to wear "something old, something new, something borrowed, something blue."

Traditional superstitions are many: it is bad luck for the bride to try on her gown before the wedding ceremony or to be seen by the groom before she appears in it; it is bad luck to be married on Friday or Saturday, to look into a mirror after gowned, to see a coffin in the sight of a bridal party. The day she selects for the wedding is important:

Monday for wealth
Tuesday for health;
Wednesday's the best day of all;
Thursday for crosses,
Friday for losses
and Saturday no luck at all.

The bride will prefer June month for her wedding. June is in honor of Juno, sister and wife of Jupiter, goddess of marriage and women's protector. May is regarded as an unlucky month.

Married in January's hoar and rime
Widowed you'll be before your prime.
Married in February's sleepy weather
Life you'll tread in time together.
Married when March winds shrill and roar
Your home will be on a distant shore.
Married 'neath April's changeful skies
A checquered path before you lies.
Married when bees o'er May blossoms flit

Strangers around your board will sit.
Married in month of roses—June
Life will be one long honeymoon.
Married in July with flowers ablaze
Bitter-sweet memories on after days.
Married in August's heat and drowse
Lover and friend in your chosen spouse.
Married in September's golden glow
Smooth and serene your life will go.
Married when leaves in October thin
Toil and hardship for you begin.
Married in veils of November mist
Fortune your wedding ring has kissed.
Married in days of December cheer
Love's star shines brighter from year to year.

"Unhappy is the bride that the rain falls on."
See groom; jumping out of bed; marriage; sewing; shoes; sneezing; wedding, approaching; white.

bridegroom:
An old superstition carried on ritualistically by some strict Orthodox Jews is the custom for the bridegroom to break a glass with his foot (at the wedding ceremony). The whole company then shouts "Mazel tov" or "Good Luck."
See groom.

bride's bouquet:
This, decorated with ribbons, must be tied in knots to hold the good wishes of the bride's friends.
The girl catching the bouquet will be the next one married. She must make a wish for the bride which will become true as she unties one of the knots.

bride's first kiss:
The groom should be the first to kiss the bride to seal the

34

pledges made. But the bride will cry or at least pretend to cry —else her life may be full of tears.

bride's gown:
The old verse on color runs thus:

Married in white, you have chosen aright;
Married in red, you'd better be dead;
Married in yellow, ashamed of the fellow;
Married in blue, your lover is true;
Married in green, ashamed to be seen;
Married in black, you'll ride in a hack;
Married in pearl, you'll live in a whirl;
Married in pink, your spirits will sink;
Married in brown, you'll live out of town.

bridesmaid:
A bridesmaid, by an old tradition, is expected to have the good fortune of becoming a bride within a year. If she stumbles in the procession to an altar she will have the bad luck of becoming an old maid.

If she is thrice a bridesmaid and still not a bride she may break the jinx by being bridesmaid seven times.

bridge:
See card playing.

brightness:
See intelligence.

brimstone and gunpowder:
See cures.

Broadway dancers:
See theatre.

broken wedding ring:
See wedding ring.

35

bronchitis:
See Quimby-ism.

bronze:
See wedding anniversaries.

broom:
A broom falling on the floor is a sign of death. Juanita Hall holds this superstition.

See fairy faith; gold fish; moving into a new home; sweeping dust.

broomstick:
See witches.

brown:
See colors.

brush, hair:
See fairy faith.

brutality:
See palmistry.

bubbles in a coffee cup:
If bubbles appear in a cup of coffee one should immediately (before they disappear) attempt to trap them in a spoon and consume them. If this is successfully done one may expect some surprise money.

See pouring cream in cup of coffee.

bubbles in detergents:
The presence of bubbles in detergents indicates cleansing powers. (In many detergents the presence of bubbles does not indicate detergent activity. Some detergents, highly effective, do not produce bubbles at all.)

buck-eye:
See horse chestnut.

buckshot:
See cures.

bull, mad:
See looking into the eyes.

bulls see red:
Bulls are said to become furious when an object (such as red cloth) is waved in front of them. Experiments show that bulls will react in the same manner in the presence of waving white cloths. The waving, not the color, teases the bull into fury. "Seeing red," thus, is a metaphor not to be taken literally (in terms of the fury of a bull).

Bunyan, Paul:
See oil.

burials:
See grave; mounds; phobias.

Burkmer, Lucius:
See Quimby-ism.

burning a hole in a dress:
This is a sign that someone is lying about the person.

burning bread:
See omens, bad.

burning in the ear:
See ears, ringing or burning in the.

burning of a house:
See house burning.

burning of candles:
See candle.

burning sassafras:
See sassafras.

burns:
See cures; words.

bush planting:
See spitting.

business:
See money; shooting stars and comets; speculation.

butter:
See bread; bread falling; buttercup; churning; fairy faith; waiters at tables.

buttercup:
A buttercup held under a chin casting a yellow shadow shows a love for butter. (New England).

butterfly:
If a butterfly gets into a house this is an omen of an impending wedding. See weather prognostication.

buttoning a coat:
If you button your coat wrong you will have bad luck on that day (New England).

buttons:
See hooks and eyes.

buttons on shirts:
See shirts.

buying a horse:
See horse buying.

buzzard medicine:
See cures.

Byron, Lord:
See hair.

C

cabbage:

It was believed that cabbage must be cooked for several hours because of the superstitious notion that it was a vegetable that "acted up" (difficult to digest). Today cabbage is cooked seven minutes (to preserve vitamins and minerals).

March 17th, St. Patrick's Day, is the exact time to plant cabbages if you expect success. (Pennsylvania)

cake:

When a piece of cake is taken and set on one's plate and then tips over on its side—this is a sign of bad luck (New England).

See baking; blowing out birthday candles; clockwise; wedding cake.

calamity:

See tragedy.

Caldwell, Charles:

See phrenology.

calf:

See cow.

camphor:

See boils; colds.

canaries:

See birds.

Cancer:

See astrology; birth stones.

candle:

When the candle wax forms a loop resembling a handle

39

this "coffin handle" portends bad luck. Wax dripping down the side of a candle ("shroud candle") forebodes death to the one towards which it is directed. A spark in the wick of a burning candle is a "letter candle" and the foreboding of good news. A charred wick remaining over the flame is an omen of good luck.

A candle (or candles) is lit at the head of a corpse to ward off evil spirits.

Candles burn dimly or go out in the presence of ghosts. (Ghosts are said to carry an odor of sulphur, a surplus of which, together with carbon dioxide, causes impairment of burning.)

See blowing out birthday candles; mirror; strangers.

Candlemas Day (Feb. 2):

If Candlemas Day be fair and bright,
Winter will have another flight;
But if Candlemas Day be cloudy and rain,
Winter has gone, not to come again.
  The (Old) Farmer's Almanack (1856).

See February 2; ground hog; witches.

cane sugar:
It is held by some that cane sugar is sweeter than beet sugar. (Untrue: both sugars are sucrose, $C_{12}H_{22}O_{11}$.)

canker sores:
See words.

canned food:
See food, canned.

cap:
See baseball; hat.

Capistrano mission:
See birds.

capnomancy:

The art of divination by means of smoke. Evil is suggested if the smoke ascends dark or dense; good is suggested if the smoke rises straight and light.

Capricorn:

See astrology; birth stones.

caraway seeds:

See cures.

card playing:

A black ace fallen on the floor during a game of bridge is the sign to play no more.

Bridge players are traditionally superstitious. If it rains on three consecutive Thursdays and a person playing bridge loses all three times he is sure to avoid playing bridge on future rainy Thursdays.

Champion bridge teams have noted that private matches played after championship matches bring losses. An American team won the world championship recently at Monte Carlo and then lost to European contestants afterwards. A British team won the world championship and then lost a private match soon afterwards (January, 1955). This is good soil for a new superstition.

It is unlucky to play cards on a table which is bare. A green cover is more auspicious. It is unlucky to lend or borrow money during a game. An old Monte Carlo superstition in gambling is to the effect that after the suicide of an unlucky player those who play against the bank will have good luck.

Sticking a pin in the lapel of a friend's coat will bring luck. The dropping of any card on the floor is a bad omen. It is bad luck to sing during card playing.

It is good to keep the chips stacked in a neat pile. This helps the player's earnings. The four of clubs is called "the devil's bedstead" and is a sign of bad luck. Anyone looking over a player's shoulder or placing a foot on the rung of a player's chair brings bad luck. A cross-eyed man at one's table will surely bring on a loss. Loss of temper is not only bad manners but a sign of impending defeat.

It is, for many people, necessary to hold cards in a certain manner if one is to win. It helps to break a string of losses by turning one's chair around three times. A fresh deck of cards is always a portent to winning (for the consecutive loser).

There is one lucky card in the deck. Touch it with the index finger before sitting down to play and luck will come. A win in the first game portends win in the third game. A certain hand dealt the player is the sign of good fortune.

To have a long succession of black cards (spades or clubs) dealt to a person at play is a prognostication of death either to himself or a member of his family.

There is the familiar saying "lucky at cards, unlucky in love." This, of course, is without foundation. Probably the saying arose from someone whose love affair was at low ebb during the time card playing was bringing success. The reverse statement is sometimes heard: "unlucky at cards, lucky in love."

See cleromancy; clockwise.

carnelian:
See birth stones.

carrying a charm:
See charm, lucky.

carrying a hoe:
See hoe.

carrying a holy book:
To carry a holy book or trinket to ward off bad luck is, of course, a practice well known. A student comes to class carrying a Bible with the assurance that he will do well (good luck) in recitation or examination. A carpenter climbs to a roof to make repairs, carrying a Bible with his tools as

42

a magic talisman of good luck. (Both cases known to this author). Carrying a Bible in battle will ward off the risk of being shot (stories of veterans in recent wars—with successful claims.)

It is said of Johnny Appleseed (born John Chapman in Leominster, Mass., 1774 and died in 1845) that in his journeys through the mid-west (planting seeds [particularly apple-seeds] and spreading a type of evangelism) he carried in his bosom a few tattered books (New Testament and Swedenborg's writings) to stave off harm to him. Walking barefoot through forests abounding in venomous reptiles did not frighten him. "This book," he once said, referring to a Swedenborg tract, "is an infallible protection against all danger here and hereafter."

carrying an umbrella:
See umbrella.

carrying salt:
See salt carrying.

carrying the bride:
See groom.

car washing:
A developing American superstition is to the effect that if one has the car washed it will rain the next day.

casting spell:
See spell; voodoo.

cat:
See birds; black cat; cures; dog; theatre; weather prognostication; wild cat grease.

catching mice and rats:
See mouse traps and rat traps.

catchword:
Actors hold that it is bad luck to quote a catchword of a forthcoming play in casual conversation.

caterpillar:
See whooping cough.

Catherine the Great:
See Hope diamond.

catoptromancy:
The art of divination with the aid of a mirror. See mirror.

cat's eye:
See wedding anniversaries.

cat's nerves:
A saying goes: "nervous as a cat." A cat, however, rarely exhibits a case of nerves. True, a cat has a coordinated nervous system which makes it peculiarly sensitive; but seldom exhibits "a case of nerves."

cattle:
See jar of water with an immersed knife; wasp; weather prognostication.

cat washing its face:
This is a sign of a visitor coming.

cemeteries:
See graveyard; oil.

chain letters:
It is considered bad luck to break a chain of letters if one receives such a letter. If one carries out the instructions one will be lucky. During World War II there developed a chain letter craze.

chair:
See card playing; rocking an empty chair.

chalcedony:
See birth stones.

Chaldeans:
See astrology.

44

chalk lines:
See athletes; ridding a house of ants.

change of the weather:
See weather prognostication.

changing clothes:
See clothing, putting on; costume; salesmen; slip under a lady's dress; theatre.

changing names:
See name changing.

Chapman, John:
See Johnny Appleseed.

character reading:
See astrology; chin and jaw; colors; fortune telling; palmistry; phrenology; physiognomy.

Charles, Ezzard:
See Ezzard Charles.

charm, lucky:
A rabbit's foot worn as a watch charm or carried in the pocket brings good luck. A penny in the pocket-book or pocket assures good luck. A "lucky penny" should be kept and not spent. An old necktie worn at examinations is a good spell.

When Jeanne Eagels played in "Rain" on the stage she carried a cheap bag in which she had sewed a lucky charm.

See acorns; amulets; birds; birth stones; circle; dogs' fat; ears, pierced; evil eye; carrying a holy book; examinations; friends; gold piece; good luck; horse chestnut; horseshoe; lady bug; moon; rabbit's foot; rice throwing; salesmen; shamrock; spiders; words. See also hex; talisman; tokens of good luck; wedding anniversaries.

chastity:
See owl.

cheek:
See dimple.

cheeks, rosy:
See bread crust.

cheese:
See red head girls.

cherry bark tea:
See colds.

chestnut blossoms:
See cow.

chests, hairy:
See bread.

chewing:
See cures.

chewing gum:
See athletes.

chicken gizzard:
See weather prognostication.

chicken house:
See banana stalks.

chicken lice:
See banana stalks.

chickens:
See mole or wart; weather prognostication.

chicken's wishbone:
Breaking a chicken's wishbone with someone gives a fulfilled wish to the one who gets the larger share in the break.
See birds.

chickweed:
See weather prognostication.

children:
It is bad luck for a child to walk forwards when sent on an errand; for anyone to use a tapemeasure or a string to measure a baby (this stunts its growth); for anyone to step over a young child (this, too, stunts its growth); to handle a child through an open window (for the same reason); to carry a child to a neighbor's house before it has been carried to a church.

It is good luck to a child if it creeps; if it is carried by its mother to a church for baptism; if it cries much even though not ill; if it is carried downstairs (rather than upstairs) from the mother's bedroom for the first time.

If an infant smiles in its sleep this is a sign that it is communicating with good angels.

If a child cries during its baptism this is a sign he will be a singer.

See baby; birth; blowing a seedy dandelion; bogy man; coughs; ears; ears, pierced; fortune telling; grinding of teeth; growing pains; learning; lice; mirror; nail-cutting; prenatal influences; rice throwing; Santa Claus; shooting stars and comets; talent; tooth extraction; wedding ring; wolf's teeth.

chills:
See cures.

chimney swifts:
See birds.

chimneys:
See New Year.

chin:
See dimple.

china:
See wedding anniversaries.

chin and jaw:
A sign of a weak character is the possession of a receding

chin. A protruding chin, on the other hand, signifies a strong will, aggressiveness or strong character. A small chin reveals cowardice; an "emaciated" chin a thinking or intelligent person; a pointed chin, craftiness; a double chin, gluttony; a soft roundish chin, a fondness for food; a square chin or jaw, self-restraint and will power; a flat chin, viciousness.

Prize fighters are said to possess a protruding jaw—but this feature is not confined to those of strength.

Character and physiognomy do not go hand-in-hand. Were this so, it would be much easier to discern personality-characteristics. The superstition probably dates to the times when it was believed that physical shape or contour of body reveals thought. See physiognomy.

chips:
See card playing.

chirognomy:
See palmistry.

chiromancy:
See palmistry.

chorus girls:
See theatre.

Christmas:
To see a familiar face in the blaze of a Yule log at Christmas is the sign of an early marriage with the person seen. To become engaged on Christmas eve is a sure sign of good luck in marriage. To be born on Christmas day is the prediction of a care-free life.

See mistletoe; Santa Claus; sweeping dust.

Christmas prognostication:

When Christmas is white
The graveyard is lean
But fat is the graveyard
When Christmas is green. (New England)

If the sun shines through the limbs of apple trees on Christmas Day, a good crop of fruit may be expected next year (New England).

Christmas pudding:
See stirring the Christmas pudding.

church grounds:
See oil.

churning:
During churning repeat: "Come, Butter, Come" and the churning will proceed more rapidly. (North Carolina) The ugliest face peering into a cream jar will help turn so that churning is possible. (North Carolina)

See butter; fairy faith.

cicada:
See harvest flies.

cigarette lighting:
It is considered bad luck to light three cigarettes from a single match. (This superstition recalls the belief of the Russian orthodox who hold it inappropriate for a layman to light any three articles with the same flame since this is the procedure of holy priests who from a single taper light the three candles on the altar.) See smoking.

cinder:
See fireplace.

circle:
The circle has long been considered the charm of good luck. Draw a circle and you enclose good luck. (Even the wedding ring!)

claustrophobia:
See phobias.

cleanliness:
See tooth decay.

cleansing powders:
See bubbles in detergents.

cledonism:
The art of divination from words used occasionally. Cledonism is also associated with the movement of birds.
See words.

cleromancy:
The art of learning the unknown by the casting of lots, e.g., throwing dice, flipping a coin, consulting cards, shaking pebbles or nuts, or saying such magical words as "eeny, meeny, miny, moe."

clever:
See crime.

clock:
See death.

clockwise:
Doing things clockwise is an old superstition still practised by many. Clockwise: east to west, according to "the sun's movement." Card players may change their luck by getting up and walking "with the sun" around their chairs. Maypole dancers should move "with the sun" (the ribbons its rays). (Maypole ceremony: an ancient tree festival popular in New England.) When making a cake or pancake-batter or beating cream the motion should go clockwise. The superstition probably stems from the days of sun worship.
See drinking at a fountain; sun-wise.

clothes:
See changing clothes; fortune telling; ironing; sewing; spiders; washing clothes; wearing apparel; white.

clothes, new:
See new clothes.

clothes, old:
Will Rogers, cowboy actor, believed that the wearing of old clothes brought good luck.
See Jolson, Al.

clothing:
See bride; changing clothes; ironing; sewing; spiders.

clothing, putting on:
Any garment inadvertently put on wrong side out or upside down will bring good luck providing it is worn that way for the remainder of the day! (Perhaps an overtone of the ancient belief that evil spirits will fail to recognize the individual so dressed.) It is bad luck to change clothes put on wrong side. Better use another garment.
See changing clothes.

cloud:
See storm.

clover, four-leaf:
See four-leaf clover.

coat:
See buttoning a coat.

coat pocket:
See money.

cobwebs:
See cures; spiders; weather prognostication.

cock:
See weather prognostication.

cod medicine:
See cures.

coffee:
See bubbles in a coffee cup; pouring cream in cup of coffee.

coffee grounds:

Coffee grounds cut grease and are therefore useful in a sink. (This is denied by many plumbers who found coffee grounds, especially if left to deposit in sinks, actually block drainage.)

See ridding a house of ants.

coincidence:

Events of coincidence give rise to superstitions. For example, the following notice in a Wooster, Ohio, daily paper: "If you are superstitious, the first 'sign' at the Miss Ohio Pageant should brighten the hopes of . . . Miss WWST. When the hostesses were assigned by lot Wednesday night . . . [Miss WWST] was matched with Mrs. B . . . Mrs. B . . . was hostess for the last two state winners . . . in 1955 . . . 1956." (The sign, however, failed in 1957!)

coin flipping:

See cleromancy; salesmen.

coins:

Throwing a coin to a wayside beggar is to bring good luck. Throwing small coins into a well or fountain brings good luck.

Not only in Rome ("Three Coins in a Fountain") was the practice of throwing coins into a fountain an invitation to good luck. (In Rome it meant a revisit to the eternal city.) At the U.S. Naval Academy it has been the custom to throw coins for success in games and examinations before the wooden figure of Tecumseh.

Carrying a coin is good luck, particularly if it has a hole in it or if it is bent. At some places of trade coins are given for good luck by the seller, called "luck money."

It is well to keep a small coin in a purse and, if one presents a pocket-book as a gift to include in it a small coin, for good luck for both giver and receiver.

See charms, lucky; cripple; gold piece; mast, ship's; moon, the new.

52

cold:
See shivering; weather prognostication.

cold hands:
Cold hands are indication of a warm heart.

colds:
A practice of many homes to remedy the common cold consisted in padding the chest with layers of absorbent cotton soaked in camphor and goose-grease. Wearing of sliced raw pork around the neck to cure sore throat was a practice this writer has known as a child. A common superstition is to the effect that whiskey will cure colds. There is no end to the number of such remedies (which, no doubt, had some substance to them in spite of the strong elements of magic). Drinking kerosene to cure a cold has been a practice of some families known to this writer.

In Maine the cure for a cold included the custom of wrapping a dirty woolen sock around the neck or of tying a dead fish skin to the feet. Goose-grease, onions and molasses rubbed on the chest were regarded as medicinal for colds. Cherry bark tea, kerosene with sugar, smart weed or tansy tea were medicinal drinks.

See coughs; cures.

colic:
See cures.

college professors:
See memory.

Collett, Glenna:
See athletes.

Collins, Eddie:
See athletes.

colors:
The belief that colors signify character traits is summarized as follows:

Red governs love, affection or lust.
Scarlet rules emotion and anger.
Crimson is the color of animal passion.
Bright red gives courage and confidence.
Orange is the color of simplicity or ignorance.
Brown is the hue of worldly wisdom.
Yellow, of jealousy and silliness.

See bride's gown; eyes, green; horsemen; New Year; sewing; weather prognostication. See also under separate colors.

comb dropping:
See omens, bad.

comets:
See shooting stars and comets.

company:
See guests.

completeness:
See fires follow fires; seven; three.

confidence:
See colors.

confined space:
See phobias.

congregation:
See schism.

constellations:
See astrology.

contentment:
See tea-kettle.

contour of the body:
See chin and jaw.

54

cooking utensils:
See aluminum cooking utensils.

copper:
See metallic tractors; wedding anniversaries.

coral:
See wedding anniversaries.

cork:
See cramps.

cormorant skin:
See cures.

corn:
It is considered a piece of good luck to find a red ear of corn. It is to be kept until the next harvest.

An ear of corn with seven or fourteen rows is lucky and is a prediction of a good harvest.

See harvest; mole or wart.

corner stone laying:
If an unmarried woman witnesses such a ceremony she may not expect to be married for at least a year.

corn husks:
See weather prognostication.

corpse:
See candle; death; funeral procession; mirror.

coscinomancy:
The art of learning the unknown by consulting a suspended sieve. After a certain formula of words is said information is to be had by the manner of oscillation or shaking of the sieve.

costume:
See clothes; dress; theatre.

cotton:
See flies; theatre; wedding anniversaries.

coughs:
A common cough remedy in the traditional American home consisted of applying poultices of simmered sliced onions on the chest.

A child's cough can be cured by passing it three times under the belly of a horse. Pine needles and molasses furnish also a remedy (Maine).

See colds; cures; whooping cough.

counting:
See funeral procession; mole or wart; nine.

courage:
See colors; whistling.

cow:
If a cow eats the chestnut blossoms when they fall, it will dry up. Another saying has it: A cow will dry up when the chestnuts begin to blossom (New England).

A cow will not mourn the loss of its calf taken from her if the calf is taken out of the barn backward (New England).

To find a lost cow, catch a grandpa-long-legs, place a finger on one leg and it will point with the other leg in the direction in which the cow may be found.

See frog.

cow ant:
See wasp.

cowardice:
See chin and jaw.

cow manure:
See cures.

Cowl, Jane:
See doll.

crabby:
See cross (disposition).

cracking of the finger joints:
Pulling one of the fingers with the result that a joint cracks—this is a sign of having told a lie (New England).

craftiness:
See chin and jaw.

cramps:
A list of old superstitions in the Journal of the American Medical Association concerning the cure of cramps includes the following: wear an eel's skin on the bare leg and you will be spared leg cramps; a skin of a mole around your left thigh worn while in bed will relieve the cramps; laying shoes across the cramps' area will cause the cramps to disappear; cork between sheets on a bed or under the mattress will prevent cramps. A cotton string tied around an ankle will cure the cramps.
See eel skin.

Craven, Frank:
See shoes.

cream:
See pouring cream in cup of coffee.

credulity:
See palmistry.

crescent of the moon:
See moon.

crickets:
If crickets come into a house they bring good luck.
It is not good to kill a cricket (especially on Sunday).
Crickets foretell weather, warn of death, foretell good or bad luck, tell of the approach of friends.

Southern Negroes carry cricket nests with them for good luck.

The mole cricket to a farmer is an omen of bad luck.

crime:
Immigrants, it is asserted in popular statements, are more criminal than native-born. (This is not borne out by the report of the Wickersham Commission [1931].)

Crimes are said to be committed by "dangerous criminals." (This notion is not borne out by statistical studies, e.g., the Metropolitan Life Insurance Report [*Science News Letter*, March 11, 1939].) Domestic quarrels, minor money matters lead three-to-one as causes of murder over "gangster killings."

"Mad killers" are said to be "fiends," "possessed." Criminals are said to be "clever" (a superstition). (The fact is: the insane lack cunning *Journal of Criminal Law and Criminology*, Vol. 37, No. 4, 1946.)

crime rate:
See moon, the new.

crimson:
See colors.

cripple:
It is bad luck to have a cripple tread on one's toes. The gift of a coin to a cripple will bring good luck.
See lottery.

Crockett, Davy:
See Davy Crockett.

crops:
See Good Friday; harvest; moon; planting.

cross:
See birds.

cross (disposition):
See cutting fingernails; getting out of bed.

cross, sign of:

See friends; harvest; mirror; words.

cross-eyed people:

It is believed by actors that bad luck will fall if someone back stage is cross-eyed.

If a baby crosses its eyes playfully it will become permanently disfigured with crossed eyes (a superstition).

See card playing; lottery; moon.

cross-eyed woman:

See athletes.

crossing bats:

See athletes.

crossing hands at table:

See hands crossing.

crossing one's path:

See black cat; rabbit; squirrel.

crossing the fingers:

Crossing the fingers while telling a lie is supposed to prevent harm.

When two people happen to say the same thing at the same time they, by crossing the fingers, will have a chance to wish together for something that will come true. Locking little fingers of the right hand as they wish and speaking the other's name will bring added assurance of good results.

crossing the threshold:

See Kitt, Eartha.

crowing of a rooster:

See omens, bad; rooster; weather prognostication.

crows:

> "One crow sorrow
> Two crows joy
> Three crows a letter
> Four crows a boy" (Maine).

See birds; sailors; weather prognostication.

crumbs:
    See crust and crumbs.

crust and crumbs:

> "If you eat crumbs 'twill make you wise,
> If you leave the crust
> You're sure to bust." (New England)

See bread; bread crumbs; bread crust.

crust of bread:
    See bread crust.

crying:
    See ears; left eye; sing before breakfast; tears.

cryptesthesia:
    See dowser.

crystal:
    See birth stones; magic crystal; rock-crystal.

cuckoo:
    See birds.

Cumberland, John:
    See trunk, empty.

cunning:
    See criminals.

cup:
    See bubbles in a coffee cup; pouring cream in cup of coffee.

cup on the head:
    See headache.

curdling of milk:
    See fairy faith; milk.

cures:

Onions on the chest relieve lung infection. Tea is good for sore eyes. (New England)

Thistle root chewing is good for rheumatism and toothache. Peel a potato and carry it in your pocket: this is good for rheumatism. Turnip root chewed is good for a fever. Red-pepper tea and dry pepper in stockings is good for the chills. For a cough take spike-root tea or a cough syrup of fir balsam or water syruped with brake-root peth. (New England)

Grease rubbed on the soles of feet heads off colds in the head. (New England)

Salt pork worn around the neck (or over an infection) aids in fighting off a sore throat. (New England and Mid-West)

Mashed potatoes heal burns; mud is good for bee stings; kerosene on a feather heals a sore throat; a pin stuck in a wart kills it. (New England)

In New England: sulphur and molasses were taken as a tonic rite, an illness preventative each spring of the year. Hiccoughs were held to be prevented (during church services) by taking "meetin' seeds" (Fennel, Dill and Caraway). Snake ball, a small piece of stone or bone, placed on the bite of a poisonous snake charms away the poison and effects a cure.

A common superstition: to be rid of warts, kill a cat and bury it in a black stocking; bury a rooster's comb; steal a piece of steak and bury it where three roads cross; rub with a peeled apple and give the apple to a pig; rub with a stone and hide the stone; rub with a penny; tie a knot in a string and hide the string; count as many stones as there are warts and tie the stones in a bag and throw away.

Buckshot carried in the hip pocket will prevent rheumatism; turtle shell ashes will cure it (Maine). A bone from the head of a cod (pulverized) will stop menstruation (Maine).

A pulverized bone of a cod taken from its middle will cure

61

kidney stones. The bone in the dog fish's head will help cure kidney stones. Kidney beans are good for the kidneys (Maine).

The head of a buzzard tied around the neck will cure a headache (Maine).

Sumac will cure stomach disturbances. When boiled in beer it will break up colds, its gum will help a tooth-ache, its seeds will cure hemorrhoids and its powder and honey will stop bleeding. Water lily roots along with wine will also cure a stomach upset (Maine).

Cormorant skin tied to the stomach will also relieve stomach pains. (The cormorant has a large stomach.)

Skunk grease and wild cat grease will cure lameness (Maine).

Cow manure as a poultice is a good cure for aches and pains (Maine).

Pennyroyal tea is a curative for measles. So also plantain leaf (Maine).

Cobwebs will stop nose bleeds (Maine).

Dandruff and falling hair can be cured by the application of boiled hemlock (Maine).

A poultice of plantain leaves will cure snake and spider bites (Maine).

Asthma can be cured by drinking wild plum bark tea or by the tea made from smoking mullen leaves (Maine).

Hot potatoes will ease bruised nails (Maine).

A cure for fits can be had by taking, every two hours, the excretion of the pulverized gambrels of a horse (Maine).

Cow manure and milk used as a poultice will relieve a frost bite (Maine).

Sciatica may be relieved by the use of a plaster of onions, rum and neats' foot-oil on the hip (Maine).

When combined with lard, jack-in-the-pulpit will ease the pain of a stroke (Maine).

Eating watermelon will reduce fevers (Maine).

Pine bark (inner bark of the pine tree) boiled in a gallon

of water will ease the smarting of burns and frost-bites. The outer bark is good for ulcers (Maine).

Hazel nuts are excellent aids to cure sores of the mouth (Maine).

Gunpowder and brimstone are good for the relief of a tooth-ache (Maine).

Wolf dung mixed with white wine will cure colic. Teeth of a wolf hung around a child's neck will prevent fear. If the gums of a child are rubbed with wolf's teeth the child will develop sound teeth (Maine).

Beaver fat calms the nerves (Maine). The beaver is a placid animal!

Bear brains are poisonous but their grease will protect from colds and alleviate the aches in muscles and reduce swollen joints. Sleeping on a bear skin will cure a back ache (Maine).

See baldness; beads and teeth; bed bugs; bees, boils; colds; coughs; cramps; dogs' fat; ear ache; eye trouble; flies; head-ache; hops in pillow; horse chestnut; lady bug; mesmerism; metallic tractors; mole or wart; name changing; a Quimby-ism; rheumatism; spring tonic; stepping on a rusty nail; water lily roots; wedding ring; whooping cough; words.

curly hair:
See hair; rum.

curse:
See Gypsy Robe; Hope diamond; nose itching.

curtain:
See theatre.

customer, one-armed:
See waiters at tables.

cutting:
See peeling an apple.

cutting finger nails:
It is bad luck to cut finger nails on Friday or Sunday. "It

63

is better you were never born, Than on the Sabbath pare hair or horn."

The finger nail jingle for the days of the week runs as follows:

> Cut them on Monday, cut them for wealth,
> Cut them on Tuesday, cut them for health,
> Cut them on Wednesday, cut them for news,
> Cut them on Thursday, a new pair of shoes,
> Cut them on Friday, cut them for woe,
> Cut them on Saturday, a journey to go,
> Cut them on Sunday, cut them for evil,
> And be all the week as cross as the Devil.

cutting hair:
> See hair.

cutting nails:
> See nail cutting.

cycle:
> See fires follow fires.

D

dactyliomancy:
The art of divination using a ring (generally suspended by a string and rotating, stopping at some marked letters to indicate answers to queries).

daisy:
See fortune telling.

dance:
See snake dance.

dancers:
See theatre.

dandelion:
The failure to dislodge seeds from a dandelion glob blown upon by three blows of breath is the sign "Your mother wants you." (New England)
See blowing a seedy dandelion; weather prognostication.

dandruff:
See cures.

danger:
See sneezing.

dangerous criminals:
See crime.

dark hair:
See New Year.

darkness:
See bogy man; phobias; sweeping dust.

dark skinned people:
See sunstroke.

da Vinci, Leonardo:
See moving into a new home.

Davy Crockett:
A name in American folklore which has had a recent vogue among children in America. A hero in a stage play (1831) *The Lion of the West*, Colonel Nimrod Wildtire, bore a resemblance to the glamorous Davy Crockett (1786-1836), member of Congress. In an anonymous *Sketches and Eccentricities of Col. David Crockett of West Tennessee* (1833) some of the best folk stories of this hero appeared. Crockett himself wrote an autobiography. The lore revolves around a career of a backwoodsman's progress from an Indian fighter and bear hunter to a "coonskin Congressman" and Texan patriot.

Crockett died at the Alamo and became a legend. Here superstition mingles with humorous myth, in the legends of a hunter whose strength is the match for any animal. The animals sighed relief when Crockett died. Rattlesnakes frolicked with joy. Men drop tears at the sight of his old fox-skin cap hanging on the cabin wall.

Children emulate Davy Crockett's antics, the coonskin cap becoming the emblem of prowess and daring. Pent-up emotions explode into acceptable expressions of behavior of cunning and unlicensed bravery.

day, wedding:
See wedding day.

days of the week:
In Maine folklore the workdays of the week are graded thus:

> Monday for health
> Tuesday for wealth

Wednesday the best day of all
Thursday for crosses
Friday for losses
Saturday no luck at all.

See under separate days; bride; moving into a new home.

dead:
See burials; dreams; funerals; grave.

death:
It is common to open the doors and windows of the room in which a sick person has just died. This is not only a procedure for room-airing but a gesture to permit the departing spirit free flight. A plate of salt placed in the room is a purger of the sins of the deceased.

The clock is usually stopped when a member of the family dies (North Carolina and elsewhere). This practice probably stems from an earlier period (when clocks were rare and costly)when the head of the house tended the winding of the clock. His death left the clock unattended. In New York and New Hampshire and other places (from a European source) the superstition developed that bad luck would come to the house unless the clock is stopped—to limit the power of death.

See Christmas prognostication; corpse; dying; evil eye; "fatal 20" superstition; feathers; fires follow fires; funeral; palmistry; phobias; sleep walking; sneezing; theatre; travelling; voodoo.

death, signs of approaching:
Several types of circumstance have been popularly considered as signs of approaching death: a howling dog, the ticking of a death-watch (small insect which creeps on wood, especially old chests, drawers or boxes, making a noise on contact with a splinter), the breaking of a mirror.

See apron dropping; astrology; bees; beetles (wood boring); birds; blackbird; broom; candle; card playing; crickets;

67

dog; dreams; ears; firefly; ironing board; measuring hands; owl; mirror; robin; seeing one's shadow; sewing; shoes; shooting stars and comets; warning of death.

death-watch:
See death, signs of approaching.

December:
See birthstones; marriage.

Dee, "Dr.":
See magic crystal.

deformity:
See prenatal influences.

detergents:
See bubbles in detergents.

Devil, the:
When the Devil appears he likes to take the form of a black cat or a black dog. A black pig suits him well. (New England)

Say the Lord's Prayer backwards and you will see the Devil. (New England)

See bogy man; dimple; fairy faith; hooks and eyes; horseshoe; jar of water with an immersed knife; praying mantis; scarlet; sewing; sneezing; witches; yawning.

diamond:
See birth stones; wedding anniversaries.

diamond, yellow:
See wedding anniversaries.

dice throwing:
See cleromancy.

Dickens, Charles:
See magic crystal.

digging a grave:
See grave.

dill seeds:
See cures.

dimple:

Dimple in chin
Devil within.

A dimple in your cheek
Many hearts you will seek;
A dimple in your chin
Many hearts you will win.

A person with a dimple in his or her chin or cheek will never commit murder.

dinner dishes:
See sleepy.

dinner guest:
See dish rag; empty seat.

dirt:
See phobias; sweeping dust.

disaster:
See Friday; misfortune; shooting stars and comets; travelling.

disease:
See bachelor; cures; horse chestnut; metallic tractors; phobias; Quimby-ism.

dish:
See breaking a dish; sleepy.

dish rag:
Drop a dish rag and this means something special is going to happen. Mountain folk of Alabama interpret this to mean the approach of a sweetheart. To others it signifies an impending quarrel, a dinner guest. See mole or wart.

disposition, bad:
See cross (disposition).

disposition, good:
See bees.

divination:
A deliberate questioning of the unknown (future, powers, etc.).

See apple love divination; Bible divination; capnomancy; cledonism; coscinomancy; dactyliomancy; fortune telling; magic crystal; onomancy.

dog:
If a yellow dog happens to follow in one's tracks this is an omen of good luck. A strange dog following on one's heels or making its home with you also brings good luck. [This goes also for a strange cat.]

If a dog howls at night, particularly at the moon, this means death.

If a dog continues to roll over this means company is coming. A dog predicts rain by lying on its back or by eating grass.

Burnt brandy will stunt the growth of a dog. A dog's scenting is infallible. This is a superstition—simply not truth.

See athletes; birds; black dog; weather prognostication; witches.

dog fish:
See cures.

dog's devotion:
A dog's devotion to its master is such that it will never

bite him. This is a saying based on emotion rather than truth.

dogs' fat:
Dogs' fat is a charm against tuberculosis. The demand in New York City for dogs' fat (within the memory of this generation) to cure tuberculosis caused the Board of Health to act against this popular superstition.

dogstone:
Dogstone (herb) found in the salt marshes makes excellent love potions (Maine).

dog, the howling:
See death, signs of approaching.

doll:
Jane Cowl always saw to it that her good-luck doll, given to her at the beginning of her stage career by Belasco, was in her dressing room. See harvest.

dollar:
See money; two dollar bills.

domestic quarrels:
See crime; quarrels.

donkey:
See weather prognostication.

doodlebug:
In early Western days of the oil industry there appeared a character known as the "man with the doodlebug." Dressed distinctively he carried a shiny black box. For a fee he would seek out oil for a sponsor, muttering strange words and syllables until his magic box (doodlebug) stopped him in his tracks. Here, he pointed, is the place to drill for oil. A forked stick would sometimes serve the same purpose. (See dowser.) Such a "professional" person was sometimes called an "oil smeller."

71

door:

See fairy faith; horsemen; horseshoe; leaving a house; nine; theatre; witches.

doorstep:

See rooster.

dove:

See birds.

dowser:

One who locates an underground stream by means of a forked stick or metal bar is known as a dowser. The forked stick reacts in the vicinity of water, the base end of which points straight toward the feet. "Here's water" is the assured proclamation of the dowser.

Counting the number of times the fork dips before stopping and multiplying this figure by three gives the depth at which water will be struck. Three feet is taken to be the average length of one step.

A water witcher (or dowser) may determine the required depth to reach the water by placing a partly filled glass of water on the ground. He dangles a ring tied to a silk thread in the glass. The number of strikes which the swinging ring makes on the sides of the glass determines the depth.

Is this "second sight" (cryptesthesia)? "Yes" say the credulous.

Peach twigs are common tools in the procedure. Sometimes they are apple or mulberry twigs. Generally, the twigs are taken from the current year's crop.

Many verifications have been made of the procedure. The writer knows of an instance of such successful use of the dowser's fork in locating water (considered impossible of access) at his summer home in Wisconsin. The employed dowser was certain of his "professional ability." Geologists regard this as a superstition, claiming the availability of water at any point (providing no insuperable impedimenta such as rock formations, etc.).

72

On January 1st, 1951, a corporation known as "Water Unlimited" was formed by a group headed by Kenneth Roberts, the novelist. This group was convinced that Henry Gross (and others) possessed the powers of reliable dowsers. A book *Henry Gross and His Dowsing Rod* appeared in 1951, followed by *The Seventh Sense*, and, lately *Water Unlimited*, attributing to such powers a special kind of genius. An estimate was given to the effect that every tenth person has this power, to some degree. Henry Gross was employed by a school board in New Hampshire, a group of Texas cotton growers, and by such firms as Bristol-Myers and RCA Victor to prognosticate water (with success!).

Walter Klepfer is a professional "water witcher" in Texas but he uses a copper wire to guide him. His fee for professional advice is $25.00 and he claims the ability to detect water spots while riding in a car. (He declares he cannot carry a watch more than a couple of days before it stops [magnetism in his body?]). In the Rio Grande area he had "discovered" sixty wells in 1952.

See doodlebug; fruit trees, grafting.

dowsing rod:
See dowser.

dragonflies:
In New England it was common belief that dragonflies were capable of sewing up various parts of the body, such as eyelids, ears, lips, nostrils. In Iowa the superstition held that exposed fingers or toes would be sewed together by a visiting dragonfly.

dream-line:
See salt fish.

dreams:
If, in a dream, the mind has wandered in confusion this is a sign of an impending event. If one dreams hazily of a funeral, and a wedding (or vice versa) occurs, the principle in

73

interpretation often becomes "morning dreams always go by contraries." Dream of the dead, hear from the living.

To dream of muddy water is to be warned of trouble, or an impending death.

Whatever one dreams while in sleep under a new blanket or quilt will turn out in reality.

Dreams involving ants mean some impending frustration. Dreams of acorns portent something good.

Bad dreams and nightmares are believed to be caused by the food eaten before retiring. (The unpleasantness of a dream depends rather on emotional disturbances. Food may, however, cause indigestion (which is no sleep!).

Told before breakfast dreams will bring bad luck.

Dreaming of a white horse is a sign that you will become rich. (For some, it is a sign of tragedy.)

If you dream of lice this portends that some member of the family will be sick.

Dreaming about the same thing three nights in succession is a sure sign of the dream's fulfillment.

To dream of eggs is an omen of trouble.

A dream occurring before daylight on a Monday morning will be fulfilled before Saturday night. If it is a bad dream it will help preventing its fulfillment by telling someone after (not before) breakfast.

Saturday night dream
Sunday morning told
Sign 'twill come to pass
Before it's a week old.

Sickness will follow a dream of picking blackberries.

Dreaming of snakes is an omen that you have an enemy. Killing the snake in this dream means you will outsmart this enemy.

A sign you will quarrel if your dream concerns a fire.

A dream of falling with an awakening by the dream of a

jarred landing is an omen of sickness. (If you do not land in your dream your health will continue.) Sickness is also associated with a dream of water, seeing fresh beef, and with eating.

To dream of the dead is an omen that you will hear from a near-relative of the deceased. (Many of these superstitions are typically New England.)

See flies; money; strange bed; wedding cake.

dress:
See burning a hole in a dress; clothing; costume; dress material; hem of a dress; pin; slip under a lady's dress; sewing.

dressing:
If one foot is dressed with both stocking and shoe before a stocking is put on the other foot—this is a sign of an impending accident(New England).

dress material:
Material for a dress which is not made up before marriage will bring exceedingly bad luck (New England).

drilling for oil:
See doodlebug; oil.

drinking:
See bubbles in a coffee cup; toasting; well water.

drinking at a fountain:
It is an ancient superstition that good luck will follow if, when one drinks at a fountain, one approaches it by going around from east to west on the south side in imitation of the "motion of the sun." This "going around the lucky way" is an old Scottish custom. See clockwise; fountain.

driving nails:
See nail driving.

dropping:
See card playing; comb dropping; dish rag; glove; ice; knife; scissors; strangers.

drunkard, marrying a:
See washing clothes.

Duke Ellington:
See shirts.

dust:
See sweeping dust.

dyeing eggs:
See Easter egg.

dying:
A person is said to die more easily if his head is toward the east. (North Carolina). See death; feathers.

Eagels, Jeanne:
See charm, lucky.

eagle:
See birds.

ear ache:
A cure for this illness is to take a wood-boring beetle and cut off its head and allow the one drop to flow.

The fat of a fox when warmed and placed in the ear will cure an ear ache (Maine).

ear pulling:
See ears.

ear rings:
See ears, pierced.

ears:
An itching left ear portends that soon one will be crying or that one will be receiving bad news (death or misfortune). However, an itching right ear portends that someone is speaking well of one.

Ears have traditionally been thought to be the seat of intelligence. Pulling children's ears is "to make them remember."

ears, burning or ringing in the:
A popular belief has it that if one experiences a burning in the right ear some one is speaking in one's praise. On the other hand, if the burning occurs in the left ear the indication is that one is being spoken ill of by another person. If

the experience is that of a ringing in the right ear, good news is forthcoming; if in the left, bad news is impending.

By wetting your thumb and forefinger and rubbing the ear one may bring to an end the gossip. Pinching the left ear will cause the person speaking ill of one to bite his tongue (New England).

ears, large:
Large ears mean that a person is generous.

ears, long:
This means that the person will live long.

ears, pierced:
The wearing of amulets or jewelry suspended from pierced ears probably reverts to the ancient custom associated with belief in charms to ward off evil spirits. Ear rings have long been worn by both sexes. Sailors have held the notion that a pierced ear with a ring through it brings stronger eyesight. It is a widespread superstition to the effect that a child's eyesight will be improved by the piercing of its ear lobes. See eye trouble.

ears, running:
"Running" ears should not be cared for since it is better to allow "the mischief to run out."

ears, small:
Small ears indicate that a person is stingy.

east:
See clockwise; grave.

Easter Day:
Wearing three new things on Easter day will bring good luck throughout the year. Easter is a kind of New Year's Day in tradition. Accordingly, new clothes are appropriate for Easter. The Easter Parade, famous on Fifth Avenue in New York City, is a well known exhibit of this tradition.

Spring and Easter are synonymous. Eggs are the symbol of new life. So also flowers. The coloring of eggs represents

78

the blooming of flowers. An old English custom encouraged children to roll hard-boiled eggs down a hill on this festive occasion. The last egg to break brought good luck to the one who rolled it. The White House lawn has been the scene of this traditional custom of egg rolling.

Easter is Eastre (Ostara), a Norse deity, goddess of life and spring.

Easter egg:

If one finds two yolks in an Easter egg one is in for great financial prosperity.

To refuse to accept an Easter egg is an invitation to lose the friendship of the one offering it.

Rabbits lay eggs at Easter time (an old Teutonic superstition).

Rolling eggs or finding hidden eggs at Easter time is supposed to bring good luck (besides affording pleasure).

Dyeing eggs at Easter is a token of joy and gaiety. It is a ceremony of spring and probably a symbol of the resurrection. Eggs blessed at Easter are supposed to ward off illness. See Easter Day.

Easter Sunday:

"If it rains on Easter Sunday it will rain the following seven Sundays."

east wind:

See wind.

eating:

It is a sign of bad luck, particularly illness, if, when eating, one misses the mouth and the food falls.

See bananas; bread; bread crust; bread falling; crust and crumbs; cures; dreams; Easter egg; empty seat; food; goose; meat eating; salt fish; sing before breakfast; table; thirteen; waiters at tables; watermelon.

Eckstine, Billy:

Eckstine keeps an old trombone for good luck. It is for him the symbol of the big break in his career.

eclipse:
See birth.

Eddy, mother:
See Quimby-ism.

eel skin:
The wearing of an eel skin around one's waist will ward off rheumatism. Those who have done this have testified that they prefer rheumatism (New England).
See cramps; cures; rheumatism.

eeny, meeny, miny, moe:
See cleromancy.

egg:
See dreams; Easter Day; Easter egg; hens; flowers.

egg rolling:
See Easter Day; Easter egg.

egg shells:
It is well to break up the shells of eggs because witches ride on egg-shells for journeys too hazardous for travel on a broom.

eight:
Eight has frequently been the number of misfortune. "Behind the eight ball" is a phrase suggesting the same.

Eisenhower, President:
See Friday, the 13th.

elderly people:
See learning; memory; old people; sleep.

electro-body:
See spiritual vibrations.

Elizabeth I, Queen:
See goose.

Ellington, Duke:
   See shirts.

"ema ema":
   See bees.

emerald:
   See birth stones; wedding anniversaries.

emotions:
   See prenatal influences.

empty seat:
   It is considered bad luck to leave a seat vacant at a formal dinner. The chair of the invited guest who, for any reason at all, has failed to appear, must be withdrawn (including the table service). See rocking an empty chair.

empty space:
   See phobias.

enemy:
   See dreams; fortune telling.

energetic person:
   See palmistry.

engagement for marriage:
   See Christmas; shamrock.

epitaphs, gravestone:
   See gravestone epitaphs.

Evans, Warren F.:
   See Quimby-ism.

even numbers:
   See Bible divination; lottery; numbers.

events, repetition of:
   See fires follow fires.

evil eye:

The eye has long been associated with superstitions, chiefly, perhaps, because it has the power of revealing human emotions. Evil thoughts are disclosed by an "evil eye" (even as good thoughts are so suggested). One's look betrays one's inner mood and character. Primitives believed that malignant forces emanate from an evil eye. One must therefore beware of such powers to influence and even to harm or injure him upon whom the gaze is directed. All over the world the eye has been considered a power to reckon with. Spells may originate in the eyes of animals as well as men and from such one must be ready to find means of resistance.

Since eyes reveal the spirit they should be closed at death lest the spirit seek out another victim (Pennsylvania Dutch).

Eyes have been painted on both sides of the prows of boats as protection against evil. Charm bracelets often found to have engraved on them the design of an evil eye suggest devices of protection.

Yawning of children has been attributed to the evil eye of some interested neighbor. Sickness is also attributed to the power of an evil eye. If someone stares at you, this is an omen of ill.

An Italian racketeer from New York testified before the Labor-Rackets Committee of the United States Senate that the evil eye was employed to keep dissatisfied employees on a job. Simple glaring was all that was involved. (Aug. 15, 1957, A.P.)

Dr. Edwards S. Gifford, Jr. points out in his *The Evil Eye* (1958) that wide-spread notions concerning the chief cause of headaches as due to eye strain or eye trouble are unsupported by reliable medical authorities of today and the presence of some neurosis is often the major difficulty. The association of a lack of a feeling of well being with eye trouble, he holds, belongs with the ancient traditional belief in the powers of vision as the primary source of disturbances. See witches.

evil, lurking:

See capnomancy; peacock; talisman.

evil spirits:

See birds; bogy man; candle; devil; ears, pierced; funeral procession; garlic; getting out of bed; hair; hex; incompletion; jar of water with an immersed knife; leaving a house; New Year; snapping the fingers; sneezing; upside down pictures; yawning.

examinations:

Sleep with books under the pillow. You may thus more easily pass an examination. See carrying a holy book; charm, lucky; coins; memory.

extraction:

See tooth extraction.

eye, black:

See black eye.

eye, left:

See left eye.

eye, right:

See right eye.

eyebrows:

In American folklore eye brows set far apart signify that the individual will live away from home territory. On the other hand, eye brows set close or meeting signify that the individual will be living near his present home. (The English have held that in the latter case the sign is that of impending trouble.) Eyebrows which meet are a sign of becoming rich. See physiognomy; witches.

eyes:

See evil eye; fortune telling; hooks and eyes; looking into the eyes; stye in the eye; phrenology; pumpkins; wedding ring; witches.

eyes, black:
See fortune telling.

eyes, blue:
See fortune telling.

eyes, gray:
See fortune telling.

eyes, green:
A person with green eyes is not to be trusted. He or she is also considered to be violently jealous.

eyes, sore:
See cures.

eye trouble:
Pierced ears are said to cure eye trouble. Sore eyes may be cured by rainwater. A gold ring will cure a stye. Fennel seed is a curative for eye trouble (Maine). See birds; ears, pierced; evil eye; meat eating.

Ezzard Charles:
Heavy-weight fighter who in Cincinnati refused to leave his dressing room until one of his handlers went to his home to retrieve an old training robe which his wife had thrown into an ash can.

F

face:
See Christmas; churning; fair of face; freckles; moonshine; physiognomy.

failure:
See palmistry.

fainting:
See theatre.

fair of face:
See fortune telling.

fair weather:
See weather prognostication.

fairy:
See tooth extraction; wand, magic.

fairy faith:
Fairies have had less hold on the Yankee mind. Whittier once observed that "our superstitions [are] . . . mostly of a stern and less poetical kind." Fairies became in New England "hags" or witches. These were the "well known" spirits who rode horses at night, curdled milk, prevented butter from churning and engaged in comic pranks and malicious mischief. Local witches haunted almost every village in New England —concentrating upon any "peculiar" individual (recluse, eccentric, surly or crabbed nature, scandal related, suspicious, mysterious).

For example: Betty Booker was a vengeful fairy-witch in Kittery, Maine. Uncle Kaler controlled the good or bad weather in Hallowell, Maine. There was the witch-weaver of Narragansett, Rhode Island, who controlled the output of weaving. Cape Cod had its "Sea Witch of Billingsgate" who rode in the belly of a whale. Many were the means of controlling a witch, e.g., a broom or hair-brush near a door will keep the fairy-witch from entering a house and a sifter under a pillow will block her operations. See devil; witches.

faith:
See fairy faith.

faith cures:
See Quimby-ism. See also cures.

falling:
See dreams.

falling on stage:
See theatre.

falling hair:
See baldness; cures.

falling star:
See star falling.

falling upstairs:
A sure sign of an approaching wedding is the experience of falling upstairs.

fame:
See four-leaf clover.

famine:
See shooting stars and comets.

farewell, waving:
See waving farewell.

farmers:
See barns; Christmas prognostication; crickets; egg; hens; horse(s); lady bug; May; moon, the new; roosters.

fat people:

Fat people are always happy. (!)
Fat people are always lazy. (!)

See bananas.

"fatal 20" superstition:
Ever since 1840 every President of the United States elected to office at intervals of 20 years has died in office. In 1840 William Henry Harrison was elected and died in office; in 1860 Abraham Lincoln; in 1880, James A. Garfield; in 1900, William McKinley; in 1920, Warren G. Harding; in 1940, Franklin Delano Roosevelt.

This coincidence is called the "fatal 20" superstition in regard to the United States Presidents.

fate:
See "fatal 20" superstition; fortune telling; palmistry.

fattening:
See water.

faucet:
See onions.

favored:
See fortune telling.

fears:
See ghosts; phobias; wolf's teeth.

feather bed:
See thunderstorm.

feathers:
Bird feathers in a sickroom are taken to be a spell to delay the death of a patient. This delay, then, makes possible the visit of a friend hurrying to the bedside of the dying person. See peacock.

February:
See birth stones; marriage.

February 2:
See Candlemas Day; ground hog; weather prognostication; witches.

February 29:
This leap year day brings good luck to the person who can claim it as a birthday. Particularly is the good luck in the area of speculation.

feeling strong:
See iron water.

feet:
See athletes; big feet; card playing; foot; groom; jumping out of bed; stepping into a house; stumbling.

felicity, a bachelor's:
See bachelor.

fences:
It is the belief among Pennsylvania Amish that fences poorly kept cause trouble between neighbors. See moon, the

fennel seed:
See eye trouble.

fertility:
See shoes.

fevers:
See cures.

fiends:
See crime.

fighting:
See quarrels.

financial prosperity:
See February 29; Easter egg; speculation.

finding a handkerchief:
A handkerchief found must not be touched. It is for tears and tears mean sorrow.

finding a pin:
See pin.

finding lost articles:
See lost articles.

finding water:
See dowser.

finger joints:
See cracking of the finger joints.

finger nails:
Broad finger nails show that a person is generous. Long finger nails reveal a lack of thrift. (New England)

Short finger nails reveal a teller of lies. Specks on finger-nails disclose the number of lies. See cutting finger nails; fortune telling; nail cutting; palmistry.

fingers:
See biting nails; crossing the fingers; fortune telling; palmistry; sewing; snapping the fingers; thumbs.

fir balsam:
See cures.

fire:
See burning of a house; dreams; four-leaf clover; friends; love life; phobias.

firefly:
If a firefly gets into a house this is an omen of one person less or one person more in the house on the following day.

Two fireflies in a house means that there will be a marriage of the unmarried in the household. Otherwise, a sign of good luck to the married couple. A large number of fireflies in the house is an omen of good company coming.

A firefly is often called a "lightning bug." For some people a firefly means death to an occupant of a house unless it is captured and confined in a glass until its death.

fireplace:

A hot cinder popping out of the fire is a token of the coming of a guest. See Christmas; friends.

fires follow fires:

It is a widespread superstition that one fire in a place is followed by two more in a short time in the same area. This is to say, that events repeat to form a completion or ending in the number "three."

Death and tragedy follow the same cycle or pattern.

fish:

A common superstition holds that fish is "brain food." See dog fish; milk; preaching to the fish; salt fish; weather prognostication.

fish-bone:

If a fish-bone gets stuck in your throat, pull your big toe and it will come out (New England). See cures.

fish skin:

See colds.

fishermen:

Fishermen have their superstitions. Fulton Fish Market is basically unchanged. Fishermen refuse to ship out on Friday until one minute past midnight. If a captain invites some friend aboard and the boatmen do not catch fish the boat is headed for shore and the guest is politely dismissed. It is an old Scottish tradition that pigs and parsons on board ship bring bad luck to fishermen. See fishing.

fishing:

When the wind is to the north,
The fisherman he goes not forth;
When the wind is to the east,
'Tis neither good for man nor beast,
When the wind is to the south,
It blows the bait in the fish's mouth;
When the wind is to the west,
Then 'tis at the very best.

(Cape Cod)

Catch a fish on the first cast and there will be no further bites. Telling a companion of a fish on the line before it is landed will mean failure to land it.

For some it is an act of good luck to throw the first fish caught back into the water (to induce other fish?).

A New England superstition is to the effect that a fish caught and not wanted should be kept and not be thrown back into the water until you have finished fishing. Otherwise, your unwanted fish will communicate to others and warn them away from your hook. See fishermen; sailors; spitting; wind, the.

fits:
See cures.

fitting a dress:
See pin.

Fitzgerald, Ella:
Queen of swing singers Ella Fitzgerald avoids night club tables in places where she appears. It is bad luck to her.

five-dollar bill:
See mirror.

five-dollar gold piece:
See gold piece.

91

flavors and glassware:

See glassware.

fleas:

Fleas may be driven away by scattering walnut leaves on the floors.

A flea on the head is a sign that a letter is coming.

flies:

A ball of cotton hung on strings in open doorways will prevent flies from entering a house (Mid-west). Cotton looks like a spider's web and frightens flies! The ball moves and frightens flies! Cotton looks like snow and confuses the flies.

In Massachusetts it is a common belief that dreaming about flies foretells sickness. If many flies get into a house this, too, is a warning that sickness is coming. In Kentucky and Louisiana a fly buzzing around a person persistently is a sign of someone desiring to see the individual. To kill this fly means an assurance of meeting.

Mackerel flies (probably snipe), according to American Indian traditional belief, are good ingredients in the cure of baldness. See harvest flies; weather prognostication.

flood:

See moon, the new.

Florida:

See fountain of youth.

flowers:

A stye in the eye will follow the picking of a flower before it is in full bloom. Poppies held to the eyes will bring on temporary blindness. Primroses brought into a house where there are sitting hens will prevent the hatching of eggs. A mandrake plant will bring on blindness. March marigolds will develop the drinking habit if looked at too long. See April showers; theatre; weather prognostication.

fluids:
See mesmerism.

foe:
See enemy.

folding a napkin:
A guest should not re-fold his napkin after eating. If he does he will not be invited back by the host.

folding money:
Fold money towards you; this means more to come. Fold money away from you; this means money leaves quickly.

fondling a cat:
To fondle or play with a cat is to invite poor health. See cats.

fondness for food:
See chin and jaw.

Fonyo, Tibor:
See jewelry.

food:
See aluminum cooking utensils; brain food; dreams; eating; grape seeds; meat eating; milk; sauerkraut.

food, canned:
It is commonly held that any left-overs from an open can should be placed in a glass jar before placing them in a refrigerator. (This idea prevails in spite of the absence of hazard in modern manufacturing. The United States Department of Agriculture asserts that food may remain in the can if the can is kept cool and covered.) Widely held has been the notion that food left in a can will turn poisonous after the can is opened unless immediately taken out.

food, fondness for:
See chin and jaw.

foot:

See bridegroom; dressing; feet; rabbit's foot; left foot; right foot.

foot itching:

If the bottom of the foot itches, this is a sign that you will be walking in strange places or strange lands (New England).

forehead, high:

See phrenology.

fore-telling:

See fortune telling; future predictions; scapulimancy; three; weather prognostication; witches.

forgetting:

If an article is forgotten at home and one returns for it this is unlucky. To counteract this spell one should sit down before venturing out again (to break the spell).

forgetting while relating:

To forget in the midst of relating is a sign of lying.

fork:

See knife; knife and fork; strangers.

fortune:

See boasting.

fortune telling:

One's birthday tells one's fortune:

Monday's child is fair of face,
Tuesday's child is full of grace,
Wednesday's child is sorry and sad,
Thursday's child is merry and glad,
Friday's child is loving and giving,
And Saturday's child must work for a living,
But the child that is born on the Sabbath Day
Is bonny and merry and glad and gay.

94

Another rhyme has it:

Born on a Monday, fair of face,
Born on a Tuesday, full of God's grace,
Born on a Wednesday, merry and glad,
Born on a Thursday, sour and sad,
Born on a Friday, godly given,
Born on a Saturday, work for a living,
Born on a Sunday, never shall want,
So there's the week and the end on't.

(New England)

Ask a daisy any question that can be answered by a Yes or No. One by one pull off the petals, for the first say Yes, the second, No, etc. The last petal will give the answer.

Your fortune can be told by your finger nails. Say the following rhyme:

A friend
A foe
A gift
A beau
A journey to go.

While each item is said touch each finger-tip with the corresponding tip of the other hand, beginning with the thumb. The white marks on the nails will give the clue. The number of white marks on the nails will indicate the number of lies told. (New England)

One may read character in a person's eyes:

Gray eyes, greedy,
Blue eyes, beauty,
Black eyes, pig-a-pies,
Sure to tell lies.

or,

Black eyes, tell lies,
Blue eyes, pick pies,
Gray eyes, greedy gut,
Eat all the world up.

or,

Blue eyes, pick pies,
Turn around and tell lies,
Gray eyes, greedy gut
Eat all the world up. (New England)

Fortune telling by the break of a hair proceeds as follows:
Pull a hair from your head. Then give it to a friend. Clasp
your hands so that the two fore-fingers meet upright, touching lightly. Ask your friend to pass the hair between the
finger tips. When the hair goes down, say "A", then when
it passes further say "B". The letter at which the hair breaks
is the initial of your future marriage partner. (New England)

Buttons are common vehicles of telling fortunes. Well
known sayings are repeated:

"Rich man, poor man, beggar man, thief,
Doctor, lawyer, merchant, chief."

The above is a prophecy of a child's future occupation.
Each button is named by one occupation in this lingo, the
list is gone through and the last button names the station in
life.

So, in similar procedure, buttons are counted off to indicate what is expected, e.g., "Silks, satins, calico, rags"—which
kind of clothes to wear; "Coach, carriage, wheelbarrow, cart"
—which manner of riding; "Horse, cow, pig, sheep"—which
animal is to draw the vehicle; "Big house, little house, pigpen,

barn"—which type of house is to be lived in; "Palace, mansion, cottage, hut"—similarly. The wedding ring to be worn is to be foretold by saying "Gold, silver, diamond, brass" and the last button answers. Sometimes daisies are used instead of buttons. (New England) See apple love divination; astrology; birthday; divination; gypsies; letter prognostication; onomancy; palmistry; petals, white weed; prognostication; witches.

fountain:

See coins; drinking at a fountain.

fountain of youth:

At one time the superstition was widely held in many lands that somewhere is to be found a fountain which would heal all ills, relieve evils, give fecundity and length of vibrant life. What is now the state of Florida was discovered by Ponce de León whose explorations were motivated by a quest for the fountain of youth. Water, especially fresh spring water, has always fascinated man, producing in him reverence and optimism.

four:

Among American Indians the number four was sacred. Ceremonial performances frequently employed this number—ceremonial songs sung in groups of four. In the Old Testament also among the Hebrews four appears frequently: four winds of heaven, four horns, four wings (Ezekiel, Daniel).

There is now a "four-square" gospel! See crows; witches.

four-leaf clover:

This is a token of good luck. It may indicate two crossed sticks such as are employed to produce fire. The discovery of a way to make fire by friction was, of course, most fortunate and its association with good luck obvious.

The old saying about the four-leaf clover goes like this:

One leaf for fame
One leaf for wealth

And one leaf for a faithful lover
And one leaf to bring glorious health
Are all in a four-leaf clover.

If a young lady pins a four-leaf clover over the door, the first unmarried man who enters the door will become her husband.

If the young lady eats a four-leaf clover or places it in her shoe she will discover her husband in the first unmarried man she meets. (New England)

fourteen:
See corn.

foxes:
See weather prognostication.

fox fat:
See cures.

Fox sisters:
See rappings.

freckles:
To get rid of freckles go to a brook, catch a frog and rub him alive over your face (New England).

French Lick Springs:
See Friday, the 13th.

Friday:
Friday is regarded by many as an unlucky day. There are those who (e.g. in northern Wisconsin) will not begin a new task on a Friday. A journey begun on that day will end in some disaster.

See bride; days of the week; cutting finger nails; fishermen; fortune telling; Good Friday; marriage; moving into a new home; nail cutting; sailors; sneezing; sweeping dust; weather prognostication.

Friday, the 13th:

Probably the most widely spread superstition concerns Friday, the 13th. This is the day of misfortune. On this day and date some people refrain from undertaking anything of importance, some businesses postpone the concluding of "deals," some will be suspicious of foods particularly at restaurants, some will avoid as wedding days, etc.

Among Christians, Friday has been traditionally regarded as a marked day. At the Last Supper prior to the betrayal, thirteen sat together. Scandinavian legends carry the story of twelve gods together feasting who were intruded upon by Luki, the murderer of Balder, one of the twelve.

Fear of "thirteen" is known as triskaidekaphobia (see phobias). Ocean liners have been held in dock until after midnight of Friday, the thirteenth to accommodate such fear.

French Lick Springs, Indiana, decreed that all black cats must wear bells on this day and date.

There is a National Society of Thirteen Against Superstition, Prejudice and Fear, founded in 1946, which meets every Friday, the 13th, ending its lunches with mirror-breaking and salt-spilling ceremonies. Black cats are welcome. (London has a Thirteen Club to challenge the superstition.) Lucky 13 Club, composed of Missouri's 13 presidential electors, made President Eisenhower an honorary president of the club, pointing out that the name of Ike Eisenhower adds up to 13 letters. See Anti-Superstition Society; thirteen.

friends:

If you want friends, wear a topaz (a common superstition). Two persons kindling a fire together foretells a break in their friendship. Two persons washing hands in the same basin, using the same towel at the same time, will soon be friends no longer. Poker and tongs both hanging on the same side of the fireplace means a breaking of some friendship.

To counteract such bad omens of continuing friendship, make the sign of a cross with the thumb. See absence makes the heart grow fonder; crickets; Easter egg; fortune telling; knife; glove; pin; powder spilling; praying mantis; toasting; travelling; waving farewell.

fright:
See hair; nose itching.

frog:
An American saying is that if one kills a frog the cow will give bloody milk.

What you are doing when in the spring you hear the first frog, this same thing you will be doing much of the year (New England). See freckles; mole or wart; weather prognostication.

front teeth:
See teeth.

frost:
See katydid.

frost bite:
See cures.

frozen meat:
See meat eating.

fruit:
See Christmas prognostication.

fruit seeds:
See grape seeds.

fruit stains:
Fruit stains, it has been held, cannot be removed until the season of the fruit involved is over.

fruit tree bearing:
An American farm superstition says that if a fruit tree does not bear fruit, it will help if a peg or nail is driven into the tree.

100

fruit trees, grafting:

This is "a gift" reserved only for certain people (like "witching for water"). A superstition expressed by a Pennsylvania farmer. See dowser; talent.

fulfillment of a wish:

See robin.

full moon:

See moon, the new.

Fulton Fish Market:

See fishermen.

funeral:

See corpse; dreams.

funeral procession:

It is considered bad luck to count the carriages or cars in a funeral procession.

It is unlucky to meet a funeral procession. To counteract the impending bad luck, take off your hat. (Evil spirits hovering around the corpse will delight in this show of respect and offer no harm?) (An inherited English superstition.)

future prediction:

See divination; foretelling; hepatoscopy; prognostication; scapulimancy.

G

Gall, Franz J.:
See phrenology.

gambling:
See card playing.

gangster killings:
See crime.

gardening:
See potatoes, planting.

garden seeds:
See Good Friday.

Garfield, James A.:
See "fatal 20" superstition.

garlic:
Hanging garlic around the house is a Scottish superstition: garlic prevents evil spirits from entering.

garments:
See clothes.

garnet:
See birth stones; wedding anniversaries.

gay:
See fortune telling.

geese:
See goose; weather prognostication.

102

Gemini:
See astrology; birth stones.

gems:
See stones.

generosity:
See ears, large; finger nails; fortune telling.

genius:
See talent.

germs, dread of:
See phobias.

Gesundheit:
See sneezing.

getting out of bed:
Play safe and get out of bed that faces north and south from the right side, being careful not to sing before breakfast. (Sneezing is not hazardous.) The north-side position of the bed probably dates back to the time when it was believed that the poles of the earth give off beneficial magnetism. The left side (in Latin *sinister*) attracts malevolent forces. The right side is always on the side of good luck. Always get up with the right foot foremost. The wrong foot (left) first out of bed will make you cross all the day.

See jumping out of bed; sing before breakfast.

ghosts:
Ghosts lurk in graveyards after nightfall—a superstition filled with fear and held by many. See candle.

gift:
See birth stones; coins; fortune telling; glove; knife; Santa Claus; wedding anniversaries.

Gillespie, Dizzy:
See shoes.

103

Gillette, William:
See theatre.

girls, red head:
See hair; harvest; ladders; marriage prospects; name changing; owl; red head girls.

glad:
See fortune telling.

glaring:
See evil eye.

glass:
See breaking a glass; mirror; toasting; wedding anniversaries.

glassware:
It is the contention of some bar-tenders that glasses used for beer must never be used for other liquids, such as gasoline or milk. It is claimed that glass retains the flavor of the liquids contained in them after washing. (This is scarcely true, since glass is non-porous.)

glove:
Picking up a glove is to risk bad luck.

To give someone a glove is to invite the break-up of a friendship.

Dropping a glove brings bad luck.

glove (pitcher's):
See athletes.

gluttony:
See chin and jaw.

gnats:
See weather prognostication.

goat:
See witches.

104

Gobbler's Knob:
See ground hog.

goblins:
See bogy man.

going for a ride:
See journey; pin; scratch on the back of the hand.

gold:
See wedding anniversaries; wedding ring.

gold fish:
Gold fish is associated with bad luck. Juanita Hall of the stage hit "South Pacific" has a deathly fear of gold fish. While placing a bowl full of them on the mantel she slipped, the accident costing her the singing job she held and a prolonged period of inactivity. See birds.

gold piece:
A gold piece (particularly a five-dollar piece) is a lucky coin and is generally laid away in a drawer to be handed down as an heirloom (New England).

golfers:
See athletes; tokens of good luck.

good-bye:
See waving farewell.

good disposition:
See disposition, good.

good fortune:
See boasting; onomancy.

Good Friday:
Good Friday is the year's best day for the weaning of babies.

Breaking pottery on Good Friday is an omen of good luck. One's house will be spared of damage for the year.

It is held by some people that it is unlucky to plant garden seeds and potatoes on Good Friday. However, there is the contrary superstition that Good Friday planting of potatoes will bring a good crop. (Western U.S.A.)

"The sun never shines bright on Good Friday." See moon.

good luck:
See luck, good.

good news:
See bees; candle; ears burning or ringing.

good omens:
See omens, good.

good spirits:
See hair; sneezing.

good weather:
See weather prognostication.

goose:
Roast goose for dinner on St. Michael's Day is a tradition (English) comparable to turkey at Thanksgiving (American). In 1688 Queen Elizabeth I happened to have for dinner a roasted goose when notified of the news of Drake's defeat of the Spanish Armada—happy news. Each year she kept the anniversary by maintaining the same menu. Thus, the superstition developed: the eating of goose on St. Michael's Day would bring good fortune throughout the year. See geese.

goose grease:
See colds.

gossip:
See ears, burning or ringing in the; lip itching; shoe laces.

grace:
See fortune telling; mistletoe.

grafting fruit trees:
See fruit trees, grafting.

grandpa-long-legs:
See cow.

grape seeds:
Very common is the superstition that grape seeds (or seeds of fruits) if eaten will cause appendicitis (which, in fact, is caused by germs).

grass:
See spiders.

grass stalk:
See wish come true.

grave:
A grave should be dug east and west so that the dead will be facing east toward Gabriel when his horn is blown. (North Carolina) East is a favorable direction.

Tools used in digging a grave should be left near the grave for several days.

See shivering; stepping on graves.

gravestone epitaphs:
A sure way to lose your memory is to go about reading gravestone epitaphs (New England).

graveyard:
See cemeteries; Christmas prognostication; ghosts; gravestone epitaphs.

gray:
See star-sapphire, gray; weather prognostication.

gray eyes:
See fortune telling.

gray hair:
See hair.

gray horse:
See horse.

grease:
See cures.

greedy:
See fortune telling.

green:
See black; card playing; weather prognostication.

green bough:
See moving into a new home.

green eyes:
See eyes, green.

grinding of teeth:
Anxious adults believe that the grinding of teeth by children while sleeping is an indication that they have "worms." See "worms."

groom:
Carrying the bride across the threshold is a practice not without significance to good luck. Some hold that the proper foot should enter first (but there is disagreement as to *which* foot). See bride; bridegroom; lady bug; shoes; sneezing.

Gross, Henry:
See dowser.

ground hog:
The idea has long persisted that if a ground hog sees his shadow on Feb. 2 at high noon he will crawl back to his winter hibernation for another six weeks, thus predicting a delayed spring. If he does not see his shadow he will not return to his burrow, thus foreshadowing an early spring.

The superstition is associated with the ancient Candlemas legend. Candlemas falls on Feb. 2 when a religious festival of candles was celebrated. "If Candlemas day is bright and clear, there'll be two winters in the year."

German settlers in Pennsylvania settled on the ground hog as a wise animal to predict weather. In 1898 seven men from Punxsutawney community (100 miles northeast of Pittsburgh) decided to ascend a hill to drink beer and eat ground hog. The event proved so satisfying that they pledged themselves to repeat each year. They became known as the ground hog club. Celebrations came to be held on Feb. 2 and ground hog predictions on the weather became a part of the growing lore of the festivity. The Punxsutawney stag club came to national prominence. Gobbler's Knob—as the hill is known by—is referred to as "the weather capitol of the world." See Candlemas Day (Feb. 2). Also see seeing one's shadow.

grounds, coffee:
See coffee grounds.

growing pains:
It is commonly held that "growing pains" are the natural accompaniment of the process of a child's anatomical and physiological development. This is a belief approaching a superstition among the many about children. (Growth is not in itself painful. The pains may be rheumatic, muscular or other more serious disturbances requiring professional diagnosis.)

grow tall:
See well water.

grow up:
See biting nails; tickling babies.

grow up hideous:
See thumbs.

growth, stunting:
See smoking.

guests:
See bread falling; dish rag; empty seat; fireplace; fishermen; firefly; folding a napkin; hand itching; knife; leaving a house; rooster; sleepy; sneezing; strangers; tea-pot; thirteen; thumb itching; visitors coming.

guinea-hen:
See weather prognostication.

gulls:
See weather prognostication.

gum:
See chewing gum; wolf's teeth.

gunpowder and brimstone:
See cures.

gushers:
See oil.

gypsies:
Gypsies are a nomadic people who travel from place to place in Europe (originally from Egypt or India?). Their mode of travel usually is the covered cart and little tents for stops (seldom beyond three days). Their women are given to fortune telling. In America they appear frequently at circuses. A gypsy tea room is their locus of professional operations. Their services are sought after by those who are hungry for predictions, particularly in affairs of love. Palm reading is their modus operandi. The word "gyp" comes from their preying upon the gullible and has come to mean "to be taken advantage of." See fortune telling; palmistry.

Gypsy Robe:
See theatre.

H

hags:

See fairy faith.

hair:

Many superstitions—coming out of a long past—concern hair. Good and bad spirits were long believed to enter the body through the hairs on the head. Bad spirits were thought to be driven out by the cutting of the hair. People of today believe that hair cutting stimulates growth (although hair grows whether cut or not, at about ½ inch per month).

Fright has been believed to turn hair white overnight. (Lord Byron: "My hair is gray, but not with years, nor grew it white in a single night as men have grown with sudden fears.") Hair fibers are thought by many to be extremely weak. (The tensile breaking point of hair is about half the breaking point of steel.)

Curly hair is believed to be common among girl babies. (Curly locks, on the contrary, occur on girl babies only in one out of six cases.) "If you eat bread crumbs your hair will curl" is an old adage.

Those who go in for sun-bathing and believe that sunshine has beneficial effects on the hair are now warned by the experts that the opposite effect takes place. (Prolonged periods of such exposure renders the hair dry, brittle and unmanageable.)

Hair is believed to grow uniformly and steadily. (Experts say that uniformity of hair growth is interrupted by "rest periods.")

Abundance of hair on the arms is considered a sign of impending wealth.

The old saying "Pull out one hair and ten will grow in its place" is contrary to the known fact that from each hair bulb comes but one strand of hair. Long hair on the back of one's hand is a sign of becoming rich.

See baldness; cures; cutting finger nails; fortune telling; New Year; red head girls; rum; washing hair.

hair brush:
See fairy faith.

hair line:
A woman with a v-shaped hair line ("widow's peak") will lose her first husband and soon re-marry. A widow's peak is now considered a thing of beauty.

hairpin:
See pin.

hairy chests:
See bread.

Hall, Juanita:
See gold fish.

Hallowe'en:
See witches.

halo around the moon:
See rain.

Hampton, Lionel:
Good luck comes to him by carrying a huge jade ring.

hand(s):
See cold hands; friends; left hand; hair; measuring hands; palmistry; palm itching; right hand; scratch on the back of the hand; spitting; washing hands; yawning.

hand itching:
An old superstition has it that an itchy hand means money is coming and an itchy left hand means that money is slipping

away. However, some hold that by rubbing an itchy left hand on wood and wishing for money will break the spell of losing. A right hand itching means that a friend is coming.

Hand itching also means that you will be shaking the hands of a stranger or that you will be entertaining company.

See palm itching; thumb itching.

handkerchiefs:
See finding a handkerchief; lending.

hands crossing:
If hands are crossed by two persons while reaching for food they will quarrel. See handshaking.

handshaking:
Shaking hands with the right hand, as is the custom, carries with it a symbol of good luck. Conversely, it is unlucky to shake with the left hand.

A sure sign of an approaching wedding is the incidence of four people shaking hands with pairs crossed.

See hands crossing at table.

hanging:
See Mason.

happiness:
See birds; crows; fortune telling; fat people; marriage; teeth; wedding day.

Harding, Warren G.:
See "fatal 20" superstition.

hare's foot:
See rabbit's foot; theatre.

harm:
See bogy man.

harmony:
See birds.

113

harm prevention:
See looking into the eyes.

Harrison, William Henry:
See "fatal 20" superstition.

harshness:
See ironing.

harvest:
Images ("kern Baby") and dolls (and even girls) decorated with tinsel, corn or wheat—sometimes on a pole, sometimes carried—have been set up as a kind of magic spell or good luck symbol for a good harvest. Harvest Home Festivals are common in agricultural areas—a time of feasting and prayer and dedication—with the background of unremembered superstitious practices. The first wheat garnered is shaped into a cross and hung in front of the granary for good luck. See birds; corn; crops; ladybug; May; moon; rake; reaping.

harvest flies:
A horde of these noise making bugs (cicadas) is a sign of an approaching war. It is also a sign of coming bad weather.

Contrary to common opinion the cicada's sting will not kill a person. It is the "W" shaped marking on the wings which has led to the meaning of war.

The cicada is also known by the name "locust."

hat:
See cap; funeral procession; spit in the hat.

hatching:
See egg; hens.

hat on bed:
See horsemen.

hat under bed:
This is taken to mean bad luck.

hawk:
See birds; sailors.

hawkweed:
See weather prognostication.

hay:
See May.

hazel nuts:
See cures.

head:
See fleas; hairpin; lice; phrenology; physiognomy; red head girls.

headache:
Stick a match in your hair, says the superstitious Southern Negro, and you will be cured.

Let your head get wet during a first May rain and you will have no headache for the year.

A cure for headache is to be had by placing a cup on the forehead with a lighted paper spill to heat it (Maine).

See evil eye; horse chestnut; moonshine.

head colds:
See cures.

healing:
See colds; cures; stepping on a rusty nail; witches; words.

health:
See cutting finger nails; fondling a cat; four-leaf clover; moon, the new; palmistry; rice throwing; shooting stars and comets; sneezing; spiders; toasting.

heart:
See absence makes the heart grow fonder; warm heart; sweetheart.

heart skip:
A heart does not "skip" a beat as commonly is said. What

really happens is that when a faulty beat takes place a trifle too soon the prolonged interval until the next regular beat gives the feeling or sensation of the organ having "skipped a beat."

Hebrews:
See four; seven.

height, fear of:
See phobias.

heirloom:
See gold piece.

hem of a dress:
"If the hem of your dress turns up you will have a new sweetheart."

hemlock, boiled:
See cures.

hemorrhoids:
See cures.

hens:
A superstition among many American farmers holds that by setting the hen on the first Monday will bring good luck. Setting hens on Sunday night will bring successful hatching. If thirteen eggs are set, twelve will hatch pullets and one rooster. Hens' eggs reveal by their shape the type of hatching: long eggs will hatch roosters, roundish eggs, pullets. (New England) See egg; flowers; weather prognostication; whistling.

hepatoscopy:
The art of predicting the future.

herbs:
See cures; moon.

hex:
(German, *Hexe*, witch.) A local American term for witch. A colloquialism: to put a hex on someone. In Bloomsburg, Pennsylvania, recently, a 36 year old unemployed laborer shot and critically wounded a neighbor woman because he believed she had put a hex on him. In Dutch sections of Pennsylvania the barns were painted red with a hex sign to frighten evil spirits. See voodoo; witches.

hiccough:
See cures.

hideous:
See grow up hideous.

hilltop:
See oil.

history:
The popular phrase "history repeats itself" is, of course, a declaration altogether undisciplined, although believed. (The fact is that exact duplication of events never occurs!)

hoe:
Carrying a hoe into a house is an omen of bad luck. (New England).

hog:
See ground hog.

hole in a dress:
See burning a hole in a dress.

holiness:
See praying mantis.

home:
See garlic; guests; house; moving into a new home; teakettle.

honesty:
See palmistry.

117

honor, forthcoming:
See praying mantis.

hoof of horse:
See horse buying.

hooks and eyes:
Used by the Old Order Amish as a church regulation. Buttons on the backs of coats or on coat sleeves were tabooed on the ground of belief that they were actually places for "the devil to hang 'somesing' on."

hoot of an owl:
See owl.

Hope diamond:
This is a supposedly jinxed jewel, once worn by Catherine the Great of Russia (a tragic figure) and last owned by Evalyn Walsh McLean (a Washington celebrity and author of "Father Struck It Rich").

The bad luck superstition of the Hope diamond made it difficult for the McLean estate to sell the jewel.

Mrs. McLean, who was aware of the superstition and believed in it, nevertheless held on to it. Her son was struck by an automobile, her husband died in an institution for mental cases, and her only daughter died of an overdose of sleeping pills. If she sold the diamond Mrs. McLean believed it would only bring bad luck to the purchaser.

The jewel was found by the administrators of her estate stored in a shoe-box (with other valuable jewelry) in Mrs. McLean's bedroom.

The Smithsonian Institution has negotiated to buy this world-famous diamond for a display in its new mineral hall (1958). The Soviet Government tried to negotiate the purchase of the fabulous jewel.

On November 10th, 1958 the United States acquired it for permanent display from the New York jeweler, Harry Winston who had acquired it in 1949 from the estate of Evalyn

Walsh McLean. The 44½ carat gem was delivered by registered mail. Winston claimed it gave him no bad luck.

hops in a pillow:
A pillow filled with hops and placed under a sufferer's bed will cure rheumatism. (English source)

horns:
See witches.

horse(s):
A gray horse is the omen of good luck. If one spits on the little finger and rubs it on the horse there will be money in the offing. A white horse may bring bad luck unless the person spits in its direction.

When the mane of a horse gets tangled this is an indication that some witch has been there and tied a knot to make for itself a stirrup. If, in a stable, a horse shows signs of sweating this suggests that it has been ridden by a witch.

If a horse lies down and rolls over, the number of times it rolls indicates its worth, each complete roll equals one hundred dollars (New England). See white horse; weather prognostication.

horse buying:
On many farms in America it is held that if one buys a horse and changes its name this will bring bad luck with it.

A horse with one white leg is weak. Avoid buying such a one.

It is well to remember the following advice in rhyme when horse buying:

"One white foot try him
Two white feet buy him.
Three white feet refuse him
Four white feet and a white nose
Knock him in the head, and give him to the crows."

119

Light hoofed horses are not to be regarded as sturdy as dark hoofed horses. (New England)

horse chestnut:

This is a charm to carry on one's person to bring good luck, to relieve pain and to cure a headache. Sometimes called a "buck-eye." (Ohio "the Buckeye State" is named from the widely prevalent horse chestnut, a long lived tree, whose partly opened pods look like deer eyes.)

A horse chestnut in the pocket will ward off disease (Maine).

horse excretions:

See cures.

horse flies:

See weather prognostication.

horse-hair:

"A horse-hair kept in warm water will become a snake."

A horse-hair lariat laid down around a blanket will keep (rattle) snakes from entering your immediate vicinity (protection while you sleep). (Western U.S.A.)

horsemen:

Horsemen, in general, hold a mortal dread of taking 13 horses to a meeting. They are sensitive to such simple things as a hat on a bed, an inverted horseshoe over a door (which allows luck to run out), the creaking of a door or the tap of a beetle's head.

An old Yorkshire superstition is to the effect that it is an ill omen to meet a white horse upon leaving home. To avoid bad luck one does well to spit on the ground.

The Hungarian tradition holds that one is more likely to enjoy success if one is mounted on a black horse than upon one of any other color. Spaniards also favor black horses for good luck.

A horseshoe is a good luck sign: four nails on one side

and three on the other add up to lucky seven, and iron itself is the metal of the gods (from Olympus in form of thunderbolts). See horseshoe.

horseshoe:

It is an omen of good luck to find a horseshoe.

A common superstition among many is that nailing up of a horseshoe over the door assures good luck. The open ends point up so that luck will not fall away. (Pointing down: luck falls away.)

It is suggested that the horseshoe symbol comes from the legend of St. Dunstan and the devil. St. Dunstan recognizing a visitor as the devil fastened him to the wall and began to work on "the devil's" hoof. Pleading for mercy, the devil promised to obey St. Dunstan's injunction never to enter any place where the horseshoe was displayed. See horsemen; sailors; salesmen.

Hoshana Rabba:

See seeing one's shadow.

hours of the day:

See weather prognostication.

house:

See beetles (wood boring); birds; butterfly; carrying the bride; door; doorstep; fairy faith; firefly; flies; flowers; fortune telling; garlic; leaving a house; Good Friday; hoe; home; moon, the; New Year's Day; owl; rats; ridding a house of ants; spiders; spider webs; stepping into a house; sweeping dust; upside down pictures; wasp; whistling.

house burning:

When a house burns, another should not be built on the same spot. If so, this one will burn too (New England).

house warming:

See moving; moving into a new home.

humbuggery:
See rappings.

hunch:
See hunchback.

hunchback:
It is considered good luck to touch the hunch of a hunchback. In Paris hunchbacks have a regular clientele among those who play the stockmarket. Players of the stockmarket seek to touch a hunchback for good fortune. The word "hunch" comes from this superstition of good luck associated with hunchbacks. See waiters at tables.

hunting:
See words.

hurricane:
See atomic bomb tests.

husbands:
See groom; moon, the new; petals, white weed; wedding cake.

hyacinth:
See birth stones; wedding anniversaries.

hygiene:
See cleanliness.

hypnotism:
It is said that only the weak-minded can be hypnotized. This is a superstition. (The fact is that there are but two classes of people who are not subject to hypnotism: babies and idiots!) See mesmerism; Quimby-ism.

I

ice:
See names; sailors.

idiots:
See bees; hypnotism.

ignorance:
See colors.

illiteracy:
See memory.

illness:
See cures; death; dying; Easter egg; eating; evil eye; feathers; flies; Kickapoo Indian Sagwaw; lady bug; pain relief; palmistry; sick, the; three.

immigrants:
See crime.

incantation:
See preaching to the fish.

incompletion:
It is held that to finish a job is to invite bad luck. If one is building one must leave one portion unfinished, however insignificant. The last brick should not be placed. This "openness" or incompleteness will indicate to the evil spirits that the building is still in process. Were it finished these spirits would enter to destroy it. Safety and incompleteness go together. See announcing a project beforehand; Saturday.

Indian mounds:
See mounds.

Indians:
See American Indians.

industry:
See palmistry.

infant:
See baby.

inheritance:
See like brings like.

injury:
See cures; words.

innocence:
See white.

insane, the:
See crime; moon.

insects:
See weather prognostication. See also firefly; praying mantis.

intelligence:
See big feet; birth; chin and jaw; ears; learning.

interior decorators:
See birds.

intuition:
See palmistry.

iron:
See wedding anniversaries.

iron, piece of:
See mesmerism; witches.

ironing:
If the tail of a man's shirt is ironed (or starched) it will

124

cause its owner to become harsh. It is bad luck to iron the backs of clothes (Southern superstition).

ironing board:

An ironing board falling across a door is an omen of death.

iron water:

To feel strong take water from a rain barrel containing iron rust (Maine).

itching:

See ears; foot itching; hand itching; left eye; lip itching; nose itching; palm itching; pumpkins; right eye; thumb itching.

jack-in-the-pulpit:
See cures.

jade ring:
See Hampton, Lionel.

January:
See birth stones; marriage.

jar of water with an immersed knife:
To keep devils away from a house or barn set a jar of water with a knife in it behind the door. This will scare away evil spirits (who see their reflection). In America this custom was practiced especially to protect cattle in barns.

jasper:
See birth stones.

jaw:
See chin and jaw.

jealousy:
See colors; eyes, green.

jewelry:
Tibor Fonyo, noted jewelry designer on Madison Avenue in New York, observes that everyone is, to some degree, superstitious even though not always willing to admit it. In redesigning jewelry he finds customers insistent upon maintaining as much as possible the original design and likeness. Their reasons are given as "sentiments" but (he observes) their real reasons are superstitious—men, more so than women. The old fraternity pin must be prominent and the same. (Women are

more eager to accept the latest style.) Rich and poor are alike in this regard. Rings, in particular, are objects of particular superstitious significance. See birth stones; Hope diamond; opals, wearing; pearl; ring.

jinx:
See Hope diamond; luck, bad.

job unfinished:
See incompletion.

Job's tears:
See beads and teeth.

Johnny Appleseed:
See carrying a holy book.

joints, swollen:
See cures; metallic tractors.

jokes:
See April Fool's Day.

jolly:
See bachelor.

Jolson, Al:
Al Jolson carried the actors' superstition of not wearing new clothes on opening night. He had his clothes made up in advance and wore them in rehearsals. A new outfit was acceptable after the opening night.

Jonah:
See sailors.

journey:
See birds; cutting finger nails; fortune telling; Friday; scratch on the back of the hand; starting on a journey; travelling.

joy:
See happiness.

127

Juanita Hall:
See broom; gold fish.

Judas:
See moving into a new home.

July:
See birth stones; marriage.

July 25:
An American farm superstition holds to the 25th of July, wet or dry, as the day to sow turnips.
See Saint Christopher.

jumping out of bed:
On the morning of her wedding a bride is supposed to land on both feet when jumping out of bed. This insures her of good luck in beginning her married life. To start such a day "on the wrong foot" is to court trouble. See getting out of bed.

June:
See birth stones; marriage.

Jupiter:
See astrology; palmistry.

K

Kaler, uncle:
See fairy faith.

katydid:
A frost will come six weeks after one hears the first katydid (New England).

kerosene:
See colds; cures.

kettle, water boiling out of:
See storm.

Kickapoo Indian Sagwaw:
A concoction, black and syrupy, sold by a Penobscot chief (Indian) in bottles as a remedy for spring illnesses.

kidney(s):
See cures.

kidney beans:
See cures.

kidney stones:
See cures.

killers:
See crime.

killing a spider:
See spiders.

kindling a fire:
See friends.

kissing:
See bride's first kiss; lip itching; mistletoe; nose itching; sneezing.

Kitt, Eartha:
Broadway star, who believes that if a woman is the first to cross the threshold on the new year this is a sign of bad luck; if it is a man, good luck. She also holds that unless one has new money in the pocket one will be "broke" the year around.

Klepfer, Walter:
See dowser.

Knickerbocker Theatre:
See theatre.

knife:
It is a common superstition that the acceptance from a friend of a knife should be accompanied by a gift (for instance, a pin or a penny) so as not to "cut" the friendship. One then "buys" the knife. Giving knives as gifts is a risk to quarreling.

It is unlucky to leave a pen-knife open.

Dropping a knife accidentally so that the point penetrates the ground is a portent of success. Crossing knife and fork is a bad omen.

Two knives and forks placed accidentally at a plate is a sign of company coming.

Drop a knife: men company coming; drop a fork, women company coming; drop a spoon, children coming. Never pick up a knife it its point is pointing towards you—if you do it will bring bad luck.

When handing a knife to someone do not open it. This will lead to a quarrel of sharp words. Lay it down if open—do not hand it over.

See jar of water with an immersed knife; sailors.

knife and fork:
See knife; omens, bad; waiters at tables.

knitting on stage:
See theatre.

knockings:
See rappings.

knock on wood:
Many people knock on wood before undertaking a project. Will Rogers, for example, said: "I always knock on wood before I make my entrance."

When one is conscious of boasting one may counteract the invitation to failure by knocking on wood.

The "knock on wood" superstition is alleged to have originated in the practice of touching wood on the occasion of good fortune in gratitude to Christ who is associated with a wooden cross.

knots:
See cures.

L

ladders:

Climbing a ladder with an odd number of rungs is auspicious and brings good luck. To be on a ladder with a pretty maiden assures matrimony. To fall from a ladder not only is a misfortune but portends loss of money. See ladder.

ladybug:

A ladybug will bring money and it is bad luck to kill one.

If a ladybug alights on a person this will bring good luck. Whatever ill one has will depart with the departure of a ladybug from one's person.

More than seven spots on the wing-cover of a ladybug is an omen of famine. Less than seven: a good harvest. When making a wish with a ladybug in the hand, the direction it goes in flight will indicate from where the good luck will come. This is "true" particularly to a lady hopeful of marriage; she will then know the direction from which her groom will appear.

A typical American saying known among children is "Ladybug, ladybug, fly away from home, your house is on fire and your children will burn." One is then supposed to ask questions to the captured ladybug and make wishes for good luck.

"Plenty of ladybugs, plenty of hops" is a phrase of charm and good luck to many farmers.

lameness:

See cures.

Lammas:

See witches.

132

lapis-lazuli:
See birth stones.

lard:
See cures.

large ears:
See ears, large.

lariat, horse-hair:
See horse-hair.

laugh:
See right eye.

laughing before breakfast:
see omens, bad.

laundering:
See washing clothes.

laziness:
See fat people.

leadership:
See palmistry; phrenology.

leap year:
See February 29.

learning:
There is a superstition abroad that a child because he is a child learns more readily than parents or elders. (This may seem true because of social pressure, eagerness to display and the energy of youth—but not because of childhood as a capacity. Thorndike [*Adult Interests*, 1935] on the basis of experiments concluded that childhood is not the best age for learning. At sixty-five the mind is less acquisitive; below forty-five is a better age-period for learning than the age-level of ten to fourteen. An adult, once convinced of the need for learning, e.g., advancement in position, salary, etc.,

will learn faster than a child even though it may have motivations at its level.)

leather:
See wedding anniversaries.

leaving a house:
A cautious person leaves a house, taking care not to walk straight from the door. This prevents "a stab in the back" by evil forces. (Hosts then who dislike you and your visit cannot vent their displeasure or harm on you.)

It is bad luck to leave a house by a door other than the one entered.

Another superstition has it: come in one door and leave by another you bring company to the house.

See star, first.

left arm:
See starting on a journey.

left ear:
See ears.

left eye:
If the left eye itches this is a sign that you will be crying.

left foot:
See getting out of bed; stepping into a house.

left hand:
See athletes; hand(s); hand itching; handshaking; moon, the new; salesmen; spitting.

left shoulder:
See salt spilling.

left side:
See birds; getting out of bed; squirrel.

left toe:
See toes.

leg cramps:
See cramps.

lending:
The lending of umbrellas or handkerchiefs is considered bad luck by many.

Leo:
See astrology; birth stones; moon.

letter prognostication:
See candle; crows; fleas; letters; sneezing; spiders.

letters:
If letters cross in the mails this is an omen of bad fortune. See chain letters.

letters in a name:
See onomancy.

Libra:
See astrology; birth stones.

lice:
A first louse found on the head of a child should be cracked, according to an Ozark belief, on a tin cup if the child is to become a dancer, on a songbook if he is to become a singer, on a Bible if he is to become a reader or preacher. The first louse should never be killed on the child's head for fear that he may become a simpleton.

Among Pennsylvania Germans a louse placed on a child's head before it is nine days old and then carried to the upper story of the house will insure the child with "lofty" thoughts when he matures.

See chicken lice; dreams.

lie telling:
See blushing; burning a hole in a dress; cracking of the finger joints; crossing the fingers; finger nails; forgetting while relating; fortune telling; tongue.

life:
See long life; moon, the new.

life line:
See palmistry.

life, spiritual:
See spiritual life.

light hoofed horses:
See horse buying.

light, moving:
See wedding anniversaries.

lighting a cigarette:
See cigarette lighting.

lightning:
See oil; thunderstorm.

lightning bug:
See firefly.

like brings like:
Saving stamps up to a certain amount will bring an inheritance of the same amount in dollars.

lilac:
A tiny lilac flower (white) with five divisions of the petal instead of four was called the "luck lilac." It is swallowed. Going down easily it meant "he loves me"; going down with difficulty "he loves me not." The lover's name was in mind as the swallowing occurred. (New England)

Lincoln, Abraham:
See "fatal 20" superstition.

Lindenthal, Robert:
See moving into a new home.

line of life:
See palmistry.

linen:
See wedding anniversaries.

lion:
See looking into the eyes.

lip itching:
Itchy lips may mean that someone is speaking ill of one (California superstition) or (as in Kentucky) that someone tall will be kissing if the upper lip itches or someone short if the lower lip itches.

locust:
See cicada.

long ears:
See ears, long.

long life:
See acorns; birds; ears, long; palmistry.

look:
See evil eye.

looking glass:
See mirror.

looking into the eyes:
An encounter with a mad bull or even a lion will bring you safety if you look it squarely in the eye. It will not, then, charge you. (New England)

The saying goes: "look me straight in the eyes" when a lie is suspected. (This is a poor test since a good liar never reveals his lying.)

looking over the shoulders:
See card playing.

137

Lord's Prayer, said backwards:
See Devil, the.

losing memory:
See gravestone epitaphs.

lost articles:
See spitting.

lost cow:
See cow.

lot casting:
See cleromancy.

lottery:
It is considered to be bad luck to hold tickets with numbers running consecutively. Intervals should separate numbers. Numbers ending in 3, 7, 9 and 12 are lucky. A number given by a cripple is lucky; one given by a cross-eyed man or woman is unlucky. Odd numbers are more likely to prove winners than even numbers.

louse:
See lice.

love at first sight:
This popular slogan fails to consider the difference between love and interest or desire. The "soul mate" idea fails to consider the exceedingly narrow limits of one's acquaintances at the marriageable age in terms of the enormous potential population of the opposite sex. (A study made in 1948 by M. Koller, and confirmed by other studies, of a limited number of males in a limited area in Ohio, showed that in the search for mates the exploration, on the average, was in the range of less than seven blocks!)

love life:
Will your lover prove true or not? Place three nuts be-

fore the fire. See whether they jump, burn or remain placid. This is the cue (jumpy, burn away or unruffled).

See absence makes the heart grow fonder; apple love divination; birds; card playing; colors; fortune telling; four-leaf clover; gypsies; lilac; love at first sight; moon, the new; nine; nose itching; palmistry; pin; rhyme making; shivering; shooting stars and comets; sweetheart.

love potion:
See dogstone.

love sickness:
See nose bleeding.

luck, bad:
See announcing a project beforehand; April Fool's Day; apron dropping; astrology; athletes; bad news; baking; baseball; bees; beggar; birds; black; black bird; black cat; blankets; boasting; bread; "bread and butter"; bride; bridesmaid; buttoning a coat; cake; candle; card playing; carrying a holy book; catchword; chain letters; children; cigarette lighting; clothing, putting on; crickets; cripple; cross-eyed people; cutting finger nails; days of the week; death; dish rag; dreams; dress material; ears; Easter egg; eating; eight; empty seat; fishermen; Fitzgerald, Ella; forgetting; Friday; Friday, the 13th; funeral procession; getting out of bed; glove; gold fish; Good Friday; hand shaking; hat under bed; hex; hoe; Hope diamond; horse(s); horse buying; horsemen; horseshoe; incompletion; ironing; jumping out of bed; Kitt, Eartha; knife; ladders; lady bug; leaving a house; lending; letters; lottery; Macbeth; make-up box; marriage; mirror; mistletoe; mole or wart; money; moon, the new; moving into a new home; nail cutting; name changing; names; New Year; New Year's Day; omens, bad; opals, wearing; owl; peacock; pearl; phobias; pin; plant; praying mantis; preachers and women; Prysock, Arthur; rabbit; rats; rocking an empty chair; sailors; salesmen;

salt spilling; sassafras; Saturday; scissors; seeds; seeing one's shadow; seven; sewing; sharks; ship; shirts; shoes; slip under a lady's dress; smoking; sneezing; soap; spiders; squirrel; starting on a journey; stepping on a crack; stepping into a house; stepping on graves; stumbling; sugar spilling; sweeping dust; theatre; thirteen; three; thumb pricking; toads; toasting; toes; travelling; trunk, empty; turning over in bed; umbrella; upside down pictures; waiters at tables; walking under a ladder; Washington, Dinah; wasp; wedding anniversaries; wedding ring; whistling; whistling back stage; yawning; yellow.

luck, good:

See acorns; almond; April Fool's Day; apron dropping; astrology; athletes; baking; baseball; bees; birds; birth mark; birth stones; black cat; Bostic, Earl; bread crust; bride; bridegroom; bridesmaid; bubbles in a coffee cup; candle; card playing; carrying a holy book; chain letters; charm, lucky; children; Christmas; circle; clothes, old; clothing, putting on; coins; corn; crickets; cripple; crossing the fingers; cutting finger nails; days of the week; dish rag; dog; doll; drinking at a fountain; Easter Day; Easter egg; Eckstine, Billy; February 29; firefly; fishing; four-leaf clover; Friday, the 13th; getting out of bed; gold piece; Good Friday; goose; groom; Hampton, Lionel; hand shaking; harvest; hens; horse; horse chestnut; horsemen; horseshoe; hunchback; jumping out of bed; Kitt, Eartha; knife; knock on wood; ladders; ladybug; marriage; mast, ship's; mistletoe; mole or wart; moon; moon, the new; moving into a new home; names; New Year; odd numbers; palm itching; passing the wine; pearl in an oyster; pig jowls; pin; planting; prosperity; rabbit; rabbit's foot; rain; rats; sailors; Saint Christopher; salesmen; seven; sewing; shamrock; sheep; shoes; shooting stars and comets; singing; snapping the fingers; sneezing; soap; spiders; spitting; squirrel; steel workers; stirring the Christmas pudding; stockings; sweeping dust; talisman; theatre; thirteen; three; thunder;

toasting; toes; tokens of good luck; tooth extraction; travelling; Vaughan, Sarah; waiters at tables; wasp; walking under a ladder; wedding anniversaries; wedding ring; wine passing; wish come true; words.

luck changing:
See clockwise.

luck lilac:
See lilac.

luck marriage dates:
See marriage.

lucky:
It is better to be born lucky than to be wise—an old Irish proverb.

lucky at cards, unlucky in love:
See card playing.

"lucky break":
See snapping the fingers.

lucky penny:
See charm.

Lucky 13 Club:
See Friday, the 13th.

lunacy:
See moon; moonshine.

lying:
See lie telling.

M

Macbeth:
It is considered by actors unlucky to quote Macbeth during rehearsals.

mad killers:
See crime.

magic:
See carrying a charm; carrying a holy book; charm, lucky.

magical words:
See bees; cleromancy; preaching to the fish; sneezing.

magic crystal:
A mode of divination and communication with the living-dead. The magic crystal, a kind of divining mirror, may be of any size, usually spherical, and turned from pure rock.

A certain "Dr. Dee," Englishman, brought this ancient practice to public attention by claiming the possession of a fabulous crystal. His seer was a certain Irishman named Keily who furnished the proper brogue of communication (spirits prefer to speak with distinctive accents!)

In Zadkiel's Almanac for 1851 mention is made of the large magic crystal brought over to England, called Lady Blessington's crystal—purchased at an American auction sale. This crystal was potent: performing four hours per day, conveying "big news" and even particulars about the afterlife.

Charles Dickens in his Household Words wrote about the allegedly marvelous revelations which appeared from "the revival of this notable practice of divination"—with special reference to Lady Blessington's crystal. (On one occasion Lord Nelson was accurately described by the crystal spirit "considering that no portrait, bust, or statue of Nelson is known to exist").

magic wand:
See wand, magic.

magnetic personality:
See mesmerism.

magnetism:
See getting out of bed.

make-up box:
Actors hold that carrying a make-up box brings bad luck.

mandrake:
See flowers.

manure:
See cow manure.

March:
If March comes in like a lion it goes out like a lamb. If it begins as a lamb it will go out like a lion.

See birth stones; marriage; washing hair.

March 17th:
See cabbage.

marigolds:
See flowers.

marriage:
The month of June is *the* month for the marriage ceremony. The month with the longest day of the year is a happy symbol of a long and successful married life. May, however, has been thought to be unlucky for such a venture. A St. Valentine's Day is a day of charm for weddings.

If a wedding takes place during a thunderstorm this is an

omen of bad luck. However, if the sun shines after the storm the bad is dissolved by good luck.

A Sunday marriage ceremony is a happy omen. Friday is a day of bad luck. Other days are more auspicious. A snow storm is a lucky omen at a wedding; although wealth may not be expected happiness will come in good measure.

Lucky marriage dates are: January 2, 4, 11, 19, 21; February 1, 3, 10, 19, 21; March 3, 5, 12, 20, 23; April 2, 4, 12, 20, 22; May 2, 4, 12, 20, 23; June 1, 3, 11, 19, 21; July 1, 3, 12, 19, 21, 31; August 2, 11, 18, 20, 30; September 1, 9, 16, 18, 28; October 15, 17, 18, 27, 29; November 5, 11, 13, 22, 25; and December 1, 8, 10, 19, 23, 29, 31. Marriage ceremony on the last day of the year is particularly lucky.

See bachelor; bride; Friday the 13th; name changing; nine; remarriage; rice throwing; shoes; "soul mate"; spinster; washing clothes; wedding; wedding anniversaries; wedding, approaching; wedding day; wedding ring.

marriage prospects:

Before retiring write the name of your possible mates on three slips of paper; place them under the pillow. Throw one away before sleep, another next morning. The remaining name is your mate!

See almond; April Fool's Day; betrothal; birds; bread; Christmas; cornerstone laying; dream-line; dress material; firefly; four-leaf clover; fortune telling; ladders; lady bug; mistletoe; moon; nine; peeling an apple; re-marriage; salt fish; sewing; "soul mate"; strange bed; wedding, approaching; wedding cake; wedding day.

Mars:

See astrology.

mascot:

See athletes.

mashed potatoes:

See cures.

Mason:

"No Mason has ever been hanged"—so runs an American folklore superstition. (Untrue: In 1824 Old John Brown was made a Mason—the most famous American ever hanged! It is true, however, that the occurrence is rare.) The superstition involves the conception of immunity.

mast, ship's:

When one steps (lowers) a mast on ship it brings good luck if it sets on silver. Accordingly, a sailor will throw a silver coin at the spot upon which the mast rests. A silver piece is often placed there beforehand.

See sailors.

match:

See headache; onions; smoking; snapping the fingers.

May:

> A cold, wet May
> A barn full of hay.

See April showers; birth stones; headache; marriage; theatre.

May 1:

See birds.

May pole dancing:

See clockwise.

McKinley, William:

See "fatal 20" superstition.

McLean, Mrs. Evalyn Walsh:

See Hope diamond.

measles:

See cures; name changing.

measuring hands:
Never measure hands. To measure hands is to warn of a death.

meat:
See mole or wart.

meat eating:
Meat eating is supposed by many to cause bad temper. Raw meat is held to do something beneficial to a black eye. Red meat is supposed to increase blood pressure.

Meat that has been frozen is said to become more tender. (This is denied by Cornell University experiments. The rate of freezing does not affect the degree of tenderness.)

medicine men:
See wands, magic.

medicines:
See cures.

medium:
See rappings; St. Germain.

meeting:
See sheep.

meeting some one:
See praying mantis.

memory:
Rubbing the hand over a bald-headed man will aid a student in remembering what is needed in an examination. (A bald-headed man is presumably older and wiser and the head "the seat of memory").

What you wish to learn by heart put under your pillow at night.

Memorization is said to be more efficacious before breakfast. (Perhaps for some people!)

A great deal of fun is poked at college professors. They

146

are supposed to be "absent-minded." To concentrate in a given area at the expense of consciousness of others may be absent-mindedness; but this is hardly the property of professors. It is a common human frailty. Professors are linked to the story of Thales, the ancient Greek philosopher, who, concentrating upon his thoughts while walking, fell into a well! Thales was hardly a college professor (though a wise man who among other things cornered the olive market)!

It is a superstitious notion that a formally educated person is the one who possesses a good memory. How untrue! An illiterate is often a person with an excellent memory. One need not be a "genius" nor even be young to develop a good memory. See ears; forgetting while relating; gravestone epitaphs; talent.

meetin' seeds:
See cures.

menstruating:
See baking; cures.

mental disturbances:
See bachelor.

Mercury:
See astrology; palmistry.

merry:
See fortune telling.

Mesmer, F.:
See mesmerism.

mesmerism:
It has long been held that the magnet has certain curative powers. Probably an outgrowth of spiritism (forces acting everywhere, especially where there is movement). "Magnetic personality" is thus a mysterious force.

Steel plates were used (as well as magnets) as means of cures. F. Mesmer (1734-1815) held that there is a "fluid so

147

universally diffused and connected as to leave nowhere any void, whose subtlety is beyond any comparison and which by its nature is capable of receiving, propagating and communicating all impressions of movement. . . . This reciprocal action is subject to mechanical laws at present unknown." Mesmer invented the phrase "animal magnetism" (which turned out to be the phenomenon of hypnotism). He developed elaborate apparatus and dramatized his procedures with settings of scented rooms, music, mirrors and glass. All of which produced excitement and hysteria in his patients.

Mesmer was enormously popular in France. The French government conducted an investigation which led to the downfall of the leader (he left Paris in 1815).

Mesmerism finally developed into a medical acknowledgment of hypnotism as a fact. But it also developed into bizarre beliefs which were mixtures of metaphysics, mysticism and occultism, appealing to the curious and credulous.

In America mesmerism became an almost household term. To mesmerize meant to subvert the critical faculties.

In Quimby-ism mesmerism found an outlet which played a major role in New England of a later day. See Quimby-ism.

metal disc:
See tokens of good luck.

metallic tractors:
In 1798, Perkins, an American, introduced into Europe a method of curing diseases by the use of two small pieces of metal called tractors. The metals were several inches in length and pointed. Moving them over the diseased part of the body: the result of the union of two different metals, on the principles of galvanism, were said to be efficacious. The marvelous instruments brought astounding results, with numerous accounts of cures throughout England.

An institution called the "Perkinian Institution" was established to make available the cures to the poor. The fame lasted six years until an eminent physician, Dr. Haygarth,

148

duplicated the curative effects in rheumatic cases by substituting a pair of wood tractors thus showing the effect of mind in the cures.

A popular superstition holds that the application of copper on the arm or the foot or the joints will cure rheumatism.

See mesmerism.

meteors:
See shooting stars and comets.

mice:
See mouse traps and rat traps; phobias; weather prognostication.

milk:
If milk is taken with fish this causes poison—held by many.

Thunder will cause milk to sour. The thunder-milk superstition is probably related to the fact that warm and humid weather does increase the lactic bacteria in the air and thus causes milk to sour if left in the open. See fairy faith; frogs; frost bite.

mind and cure:
See metallic tractors.

ministers and bishops:
Their selection among Pennsylvania Mennonites was made by the placing of a piece of paper in one of a number of Bibles; members were then directed to select while God determined by means of the Bible containing the slip with the words "This is the lot." Such a minister became "called" and was held to possess Divine inspiration (without any preparation). See preachers and women.

mirror:
A popular belief is to the effect that if a child is taken to a mirror before it is a year old it will "cause" its early death.

The breaking of a mirror signifies seven years of bad luck.

Such breaking is sometimes associated with spinster and bachelorhood.

(The Ashenfarb family are manufacturers of mirrors, some 60,000 broken each work-week. Yet this family has prospered!)

Some people hold that to find a five dollar bill breaks the spell of a broken mirror. Again, it is held that a deliberate breaking of a mirror will have no consequence whatsoever. Crossing one-self will break the spell.

Looking in a mirror by candle-light is taken to bring on bad luck. Mirrors and pictures are covered while a corpse lies in state at a home—to prevent the spirit from seeing itself.

See catoptromancy; death, signs of approaching; Friday, the 13th; magic crystal.

misfortune:
See birth; boasting; luck, bad.

mistletoe:
Kissing a girl under a mistletoe insures good fortune. If a girl stands under a mistletoe this is an invitation to being kissed by any man. If she refuses it is bad luck; if she is kissed seven times in one day she will marry within a year.

Mistletoe (state emblem of Oklahoma!) is a European shrub with thick leaves, small yellowish flowers and waxy-white berries. It has long been associated with Christmas decorations—usually hung from chandeliers. In Europe it was an emblem of grace and a symbol of prosperity. Frequently it was placed with reverence upon church altars.

mistrust:
See trust and mistrust.

molasses:
See colds; coughs; cures; spring tonic.

mole cricket:
See crickets.

mole or wart:

A mole (birthmark) on the forehead near the hair line is the sign of bad fortune; on the chin or ear the sign of riches; on the breast the sign of poverty; on the throat the sign of good luck.

"A mole on your arm, live on a farm."

With some people every mole or wart has particular significance. The causes of warts: handling frogs or toads; washing hands in water in which eggs were boiled; counting the number of warts on others.

Many moles indicate future wealth.

To remove a wart rub with a bean or a piece of stolen meat (the latter then buried in the earth during the time of decay the wart disappears). A wart may be rubbed by a grain of barley which then is fed to a chicken—a cure. Other cures are: Put vinegar on a penny and let it corrode. At the same time put vinegar on a wart and it will disappear. Rub a wart with corn, bore a hole in a tree, put the corn in the hole and plug it up. The wart will vanish. Rub with sassafras and a wart will go. Steal a piece of pork from a neighbor's pork barrel and rub the wart with it. It will be gone. Rub the wart with a kernel of corn; toss the corn to a chicken; if it eats it the wart will disappear. Steal a dishcloth, rub the wart with it and then bury the dishcloth. This is effective. There are almost innumerable "cures." (New England)

To wear an artificial mole is a "beauty patch" (and good luck?) to some women. See birthmark; cures.

mole skin:

See cramps.

moles:

See weather prognostication.

Monday:

See cutting fingernails; days of the week; dreams; fortune

telling; hens; moving into a new home; sewing; sneezing; travelling; visiting on Monday; weather prognostication.

money:

There is a prevailing superstition in the United States of bad fortune associated with a two-dollar bill (but not in Canada). This superstition, it is said, arose from the bad name the two-dollar bill got in race and horse betting. Many Americans used to place two dollar bets (normal bet) and because of widespread losses the bill acquired the omen of bad luck.

Dreaming about money is also an omen of bad luck. Good luck is assured by keeping a penny in the purse. In the right hand pocket of a new coat money brings good luck.

See astrology; bread; bubbles in a coffee cup; card playing; coins; crime; Easter egg; folding money; gold piece; hand itching; horse(s); Kitt, Eartha; ladders; ladybug; like brings like; mirror; palm itching; penny; pouring cream in cup of coffee; shooting stars and comets; salesmen; speculation; theatre; wealth.

money saving:

See thumbs.

Monte Carlo:

See card playing.

months:

See bride; marriage. See also under separate months.

moon:

Moon lore is full to the brim. Many examples abound. A maiden who drinks white wine and rose water and then looks through a silk scarf at the moon will see her husband-to-be. A lucky charm is a left hind paw of a rabbit killed in a graveyard by a cross-eyed person in the dark of the moon. If the moon shines on the lids of the eye of a sleeper he will become

152

blind. Insanity will come if one sleeps under moon light (hence lunacy, loony, moonstruck).

Potatoes should be planted in the dark of the moon, preferably on Good Friday; peas in the light of the moon. Root crops should in general be sown between the first quarter and the full moon; leafy plants when the moon is waning.

Vines will best be kept free of pests when pruned during the time the moon is in the sign of Leo the Lion. It is better to gather herbs before the full moon. This is also the time to take a tonic.

Soap is best made in the moon's light phase. Bacon from hogs killed in a waning moon will curl in the skillet.

Weather is foretold by the moon:

Pale moon doth rain
Red moon doth blow
White moon doth
Neither rain nor snow.

An upright crescent moon means a wet month (it holds no water). If the crescent is down on its back, cupping water (holding water) there will be no rain. Clouds are gobbled up by a full moon. If the ring around the moon encircles more than five stars the weather will be cold. (Or, the number of stars within its circle foretells the days before a storm.)

The moon plays a great part in the life of the Pennsylvania Amish: in the planting of crops, placing of fence-posts, shingling of barns and houses, etc. Moon observance belongs to the lore of many people throughout the world.

See astrology; rain; seeing one's shadow; soap.

moon, the new:
A popular superstition of ancient standing is the belief that if the new moon is seen over the left shoulder this is a sign of some misfortune. Probably this belief originated among the

153

ancient Romans who believed that every occurrence witnessed on the right hand was to be held as a sign of good fortune whereas if on the left an indication of some impending calamity.

A full moon is believed to affect many things: the weather, health, love, life, agriculture and even crime rate. A New York deputy police commissioner cited true records for a 42 year period which showed that "with a full moon there is an increase in pyromania." "Arson always rises with the full moon." A former criminologist for New York and New England Association of Fire Chiefs has claimed that persons led to do evil by the light of the full moon are "erratic if not pathological."

Some farmers will not make a move unless they consider if the moon's phase is right. "If the moon shows a silver shield, be not afraid to reap your field. But if she rise a-halved round, soon we'll tread on deluged ground."

An inherited superstition is to the effect that if a husband leaves his wife while the moon is waning he will not be seen by her again.

Good luck, it is held, can be insured by bowing nine times toward the moon while shaking silver coins in the pocket.

Wishing on the moon is common. It is supposed that by the time the moon's 28 day cycle has been completed from the point of its present phase the wish will have come true.

Pointing at the moon has long been considered to bring good luck (ancient Hebrews). See moon.

moonshine:

Shining of the moon on the face of a sleeper will cause restlessness, headache, neuralgia and eventually "lunacy."

"Moonshine makes a razor dull."

moonstone:

See wedding anniversaries.

moon waning:
See moon, the new.

moss-agate:
See wedding anniversaries.

motherhood:
See prenatal influences.

mounds:
The shape of American Indian mounds was customarily (not always) in the form of animals. It was their idea that the model of an animal would protect them and their dead.

In Adams county, Ohio, a mound shaped like a serpent is 1,348 feet long, the gaping jaws 75 feet wide. In Wisconsin a mound reveals the form of an eagle with a wing-spread of 1,000 feet. Many mounds are formed in the model of panthers with tails 350 feet long.

Indians tended to build their mounds near their villages. Charred stones in the shape of altars suggest worship ground.

mourning:
See purple; sewing.

mouse:
See mice.

mouse traps and rat traps:
Mice and rats smell human beings, *their natural enemy*. Hence, one should use gloves in setting traps to fool them. (Man is hardly their enemy! Experiments conducted in the London Zoo in 1919 show that belief in this capability of detecting human odor is unfounded and only a superstition.) See mice; rats.

mouth:
See eating; yawning.

mouth sores:
See cures.

moving:
See New Year's Day.

moving into a new home:
Robert Lindenthal, an interior designer, who has observed housing superstitions has pointed out that from North Yorkshire, England, the practice of carrying a loaf of bread and a bit of salt which carry good luck is practiced by many people in this country. Bread is the symbol of prosperity. Salt may mean bad luck if spilled; but tossed over the left shoulder remedies the situation. Judas in Leonardo da Vinci's painting of the Last Supper is depicted as overturning the salt. Carried on a plate salt means good luck.

A green bough on a newly raised roof of a house insures good luck.

It is considered lucky to move into a new home on Monday or Wednesday but unlucky on Friday. One should never risk moving on a Saturday. This means "a short stay."

One should never move downstairs in the same building.

Van companies have found every day in the week an unlucky day to move people and goods.

Good luck is supposed to be insured in a new home by sending on in advance a *new* broom (or a loaf of bread). But—never move a broom from one house to another, otherwise bad luck. "Housewarming," with guests bringing gifts, insures good luck.

moving light:
See wedding anniversaries.

mud:
See cures.

muddy water:
See dreams.

mullen leaves:
See cures.

mumps:
See name changing.

murder:
See crime; dimple.

muscle aches:
See cures.

musical instruments:
Among Pennsylvania Mennonites the belief was held that any musical aid (instrument) was known to cause a schism in a congregation. Scripture forbade the use of organs.

musician:
See lice.

muskrats:
See weather prognostication.

Mussolini:
See phobias.

myophobia:
See phobias.

mysophobia:
See phobias.

mystic number:
See three.

N

nail:
See stepping on a rusty nail.

nail cutting:
A popular belief has it that if a child's nails are cut before it is a year old it will become a thief.

Cutting nails on Friday is bad luck.

"If you cut the nails of a sick person that person will never get well." See cutting finger nails.

nail driving:
See fruit tree bearing; horseshoe; sailors.

nails, biting:
See biting nails.

nails, bruised:
See cures.

nails of fingers:
See finger nails.

name changing:
No girl should risk marriage with a man whose last name has the same initial as hers. "Change the name but not the letter, marry for worse instead of better."

If a woman marries without changing names this gives her the ability to cure certain diseases (e.g., mumps, measles) (Maryland). See horse buying; theatre.

names:
The naming of a ship is held to be important—for the sake of good or bad luck. It would be folly to call a ship after the

state of Maine or Portland. Such names recall sea horrors and are bids for misfortune. It is not considered good risk to name a ship with the word "Ice." Better it is to use the name of some successful enterprise.

It is to one's good luck to have a name (first or last) with seven letters. See crossing the fingers; marriage prospects; onomancy.

napkin:
See folding a napkin; waiters at tables.

native-born:
See crime.

nature remedies:
See cures.

neats' foot-oil:
See cures.

necktie, old:
See charm, lucky; salesmen.

needle or pin:
See strangers.

needles, pine:
See pine needles.

negroes:
See racial superstition.

neighbors:
See fences; ridding a house of ants.

nerves, calming of:
See cures.

nervous as a cat:
See cat's nerves.

nests:
See birds; crickets.

neuralgia:
See moonshine.

neuritis:
See sciatica.

newborn:
See beads and teeth; birth with a veil.

new broom:
See moving into a new home.

new clothes:
See Easter Day; Jolson, Al.

new coat:
See money.

new money:
See Kitt, Eartha.

new moon:
See moon, the new.

New Thought movement:
See Quimby-ism.

New Year:
A sign of good luck for the New Year is the coming of a dark man, especially if he is the first to cross the threshold in the New Year. On the other hand, in some places, it is considered bad luck for anyone with dark hair to be the first New Year's guest to cross the threshold since dark hair is associated with the powers of evil.

If a woman is the first visitor, whatever the color of her hair, it is a sign of disaster.

It is well to make sure the chimneys are clear in the New Year to make paths for good luck.

See Bible divination; Easter Day; Kitt, Eartha.

New Year's Day:
It is believed to bring bad luck if anything is removed

from a house on New Year's Day unless something has been brought in to take its place. See pig-jowls; sweeping dust.

news, forthcoming:
See bees; birds; cutting finger nails; ears, burning or ringing in the; good news; visitors coming.

nightmares:
See dreams.

nine:
If one counts nine stars for nine nights, on the ninth night one's lover will be revealed.

If, in shelling peas, one finds a pod containing nine peas one should hang it over the door. The first one to walk through the door will be one's marriage partner.

See lottery; moon, the new; words.

noises:
See rappings.

north-south:
See getting out of bed.

north wind:
See wind.

nose bleeding:
It is a sign that the person is lovesick when nose is bleeding (New England). See cures.

nose itching:
An itchy nose is the sign of a visitor or that one is going to be angry, or be quarrelsome, or that someone is thinking of you, or a kiss to be bestowed on a fool, or the true lover will be seen before nightfall, or (among New Englanders) that one will either be kissed, vexed or cursed.

"If your nose itches
Sign of fright

161

If your right eye itches
Sign of a pleasant sight" (Maine).

November:
See birth stones; marriage.

number(s):
See astrology; eight; even numbers; four; lottery; nine; odd numbers; seven; thirteen; three.

nutmegs:
See boils.

nuts:
See cleromancy; hazel nuts; love life; weather prognostication.

nyctophobia:
See phobias.

O

occultism:
See mesmerism.

occupation:
See Bible divination; fortune telling.

ocean liners:
See Friday, the 13th; ships.

October:
See birth stones; marriage.

October 31:
See witches.

odd numbers:
Generally considered to be lucky numbers. See Bible divination; ladders; lottery.

odor:
See birds; candle; mouse traps and rat traps.

Ohio:
See horse chestnut.

oil:
Among the sayings in Western American folklore are these:

Wherever lightning strikes, you'll find oil.
Drill on a hilltop, never in a valley.
There's always oil under a graveyard.

The belief was widely held that oil finding was confined to surface boundaries, such as creeks, public roads and even

163

railroad tracks. Cemeteries were leased as especially promising, and also church grounds. Here especially gushers may be found!

The name of Paul Bunyan, legendary hero, is associated with Western folklore in the quest for oil. Bunyan is the jack-of-all-tradesman, superior in developing tools and methods. He could sight a plumb line without a plumb line. Beginning in West Virginia Bunyan's name became super-man in the folklore of early findings of oil. Only two holes failed Bunyan in his long legendary career of oil drilling. See doodlebug; dowser.

oil smeller:
See doodlebug.

Oklahoma:
See mistletoe.

old clothes:
See clothes, old.

old maid:
See bridesmaid; spinster.

old people:
See elderly people; sauerkraut; theatre; young people.

Old Testament:
See seven.

omens:
The spontaneous warnings or suggestions of events to come beyond natural predictions.

See astrology; bread falling; butterfly; children; death, signs of approaching; dog; dressing; firefly; fleas; foot itching; hoe; March; May; robin; sharks; ships; storm; tea leaves; visitors coming; weather prognostication; wind, the.

omens, bad:
Popular bad omens include the circumstance of spilling

164

salt at the table, the laying of the knife and fork across each other on the plate, burning bread, hearing the screeching of an owl, the crowing of a rooster at night, killing a spider, stepping over a snake, dropping a comb, breaking a mirror, stepping on cracks in the walk or laughing before breakfast.

See birds; birth; black cat; burning a hole in a dress; capnomancy; card playing; cutting finger nails; death, signs of approaching; dreams; friends; fortune telling; hoe; ironing board; knife; luck, bad; mirror; money; nose itching; owl; peacock; pin; robin; rooster; salt, spilling of; seeing one's shadow; shooting stars and comets; sneezing; spiders; starting on a journey; stumbling; stumbling on a threshold; theatre; three; thumb pricking; toasting; waiters at tables; walking under a ladder; wedding day; yawning.

omens, good:
See bees; birds; capnomancy; charm, lucky; cutting finger nails; dreams; fortune telling; horse chestnut; horseshoe; luck, good; nose itching; pin; robin; sewing; sneezing; stockings; theatre; thunder; wedding day.

omoplatoscopy:
See scapulimancy.

one:
See crows.

one-armed customer:
See waiters at tables.

onions:
In North Carolina lore onions are associated with certain superstitious ideas and practices. A raw potato held in the mouth while peeling onions is said to prevent the juice from striking the eyes. A match or a bit of bread held between the teeth will also produce the same effect. Or, again, turning on the faucet and letting water run will produce the same results. See colds; coughs; cures; weather prognostication.

onomancy:
The art of divining good or ill fortune from the letters of a person's name.

onychomancy:
See palmistry.

opals, wearing:
Wearing opals is to invite bad luck. See birth stones.

opening night:
See Jolson, Al.

orange:
See colors.

order-book:
See salesmen.

ornithomancy:
See birds.

owl:
The sound of an owl is an omen of bad luck. (Even in ancient Rome if an owl was seen about the city during the day it was caught, destroyed and the ashes scattered in the Tiber.) An owl persists as an omen of ill fortune, "the funeral bird of the night" (Pliny). Perched on a house an owl predicted death to an occupant, thus "death's dreadful messenger." In Wales the hoot of an owl was the sign of an unmarried girl's surrender of her chastity. (In India, among some peoples, the owl is sacred since its sight is phenomenal.) But the bad omen superstition persists widely even in this country today. See birds; omens, bad; sailors; weather prognostication.

oysters:
See pearl in an oyster; weather prognostication.

pain:
See growing pains; pin.

pain relief:
See cures; horse chestnut.

painting a rat:
See rats.

palm:
See spitting.

palmistry:
An ancient "science" which foretells events and character from the shape and lines of the hand, fingers, nails, etc.

Chirognomy: "the art" of assessing the character of a person on the basis of the shape and general appearance of the hands.

Chiromancy: "the art" of prophecy from indications of the hands.

Onychomancy: "the art" of foretelling on the basis of characteristics of the finger nails.

A hand that is thick and coarse with short fingers is taken to indicate a brutal and unimaginative character. A hand square in shape suggests industry and honest dealings. A palm with fingers tapering from a broad base suggests a witty, social and artistic person. A hand that is fan-shaped (with fingers spread at their top) reveals a daring and energetic spirit. A hand, bony and irregular in shape, with protruding joints suggests a character adept at dealing with knotty problems such as concern philosophers. A hand fragile in appear-

167

ance with long and tapering fingers and almond-shaped finger-nails indicates an idealistic and visionary nature. Such a possessor has power of intuitive insight and is given to credulity and tenderness. A mixed hand (with a combination of characteristics) suggests a more unpredictable and complex personality.

Palm readers observe the fatty tissues ("mounds") and the locations of these give the cue to personality traits. E.g., the mount of Jupiter is the mound of the base of the forefinger, suggesting pride, ambition and leadership; the mount of Saturn beneath the middle finger, suggesting wisdom and prudence; the mount of Mercury at the base of the little finger, indicating a practical nature; etc.

Lines on the hand are held to be important indications of life and character traits: the line of life (the crease extending from the wrist below the thumb and extending to a point midway between the first finger and the thumb. "Long line, long life." "Broken line, accident or illness and even death." Other lines reveal ambition, love, fate, success, failure, health, etc.

Palmistry has had a long existence and continues to attract the credulous (even though there is the plain fact of purely anatomical creases and tissue formations). See gypsies.

palm itching:
The itching of the palm is a sign that one is to come into possession of unanticipated money. If it continues it is the sign of good fortune. See hand itching.

paper:
See wedding anniversaries.

parchment:
See talisman.

parsons and pigs:
See fishermen.

168

passing salt:
See salt passing.

passing wine:
See wine passing.

passion:
See colors.

pathetic fallacy:
This fallacy is common to superstitions. It implies that an object or an animal suffers *(pathein)* from the same reactions and emotions as a human. A golf stick is thrown to the ground in anger because "it is bad."

pathological people:
See moon, the new.

pathophobia:
See phobias.

pattern of events:
See fires follow fires.

pea shelling:
See shelling peas.

peace:
See birds.

peacock:
The bird of ill omen, scrupulously avoided by stage people. The Shuberts never permitted peacocks to appear on scenic designs. Margaret Anglin playing on a Chicago theatre stage remarked that something was wrong, some evil force present. Later she noticed the painted design of a peacock on a piece of furniture which had been covered over. When this piece of furniture was removed the play went on smoothly.

Peacock feathers are to be avoided since they are omens

169

of lurking evil. Never should they be permitted in a house. See birds; weather prognostication.

peanut shells:
See athletes.

pearl:
A ring set with a pearl is unlucky. Pearls signify tears. See birth stones; wedding anniversaries.

pearl in an oyster:
It is a sign of good luck to discover a pearl in an oyster.

peas:
See moon.

peas, blackeyed:
See pig-jowls.

pebbles:
See cleromancy.

peeling an apple:
In Kentucky and New England the superstition holds that if one peels an apple without breaking it and throws it over the left shoulder it will form the initial of the one you will marry. A red apple is to be preferred. See cures.

peepholes:
See theatre.

peg driving:
See fruit tree bearing; nail driving.

penny:
See charm, lucky; knife; mole or wart; money; cures.

pennyroyal tea:
See cures.

pepper:
See red pepper tea.

pepper, dry:
See cures.

perfume:
See voodoo.

Perkinian Institution:
See metallic tractors.

personality characteristics:
See astrology; character reading; chin and jaw; finger nails; fortune telling; talent; temper.

pestilence:
See shooting stars and comets.

petals, white weed:
Fortunes can be told by means of white weed petals, e.g., whether "rich man, poor man, beggar man, thief, doctor, lawyer, merchant, chief," four or eight possible husbands (New England). See daisy.

phantom ship:
In January of the year 1647 a new ship containing a valuable cargo and several distinguished persons as passengers put to sea from New Haven bound for England. No word came of its arrival. On the following June a great thunderstorm occurred, followed by a calm sea an hour before sunset. A ship of like dimensions with the missing ship appeared in the air at the mouth of the harbor for one half hour. The phantom ship came within a stone's throw of the excited spectators. Piece by piece the phantom disappeared leaving a dull and smoke-color cloud. The Rev. Mr. Davenport, minister of New Haven, declared the phantom ship seen by many to have been a disclosure by God of his providential care of those for whom so many prayers had been raised.

phobias:
Many people suffer from irrational fears often associated with superstitions.

Some of these fears are:

acrophobia: fear of height (standing on a ladder rung or looking down from an apartment window).

agoraphobia: fear of empty space or an unwillingness to cross the center of an empty room or pass in the open before a crowd or even alone.

claustrophobia: fear of confined space. (Mussolini suffered from this fear and sought spacious office rooms.)

myophobia: fear of mice.

mysophobia: fear of dirt.

nyctophobia: dread of the dark.

pathophobia: fear of disease germs.

phobophobia: dread of fear itself.

pyrophobia: fear of causing a fire.

taphephobia: fear of being buried alive.

thanatophobia: fear of death.

triskaidekaphobia: dread of the number "13." Hotels and office buildings often pass up the number "13" and use instead "12A." It is considered unlucky to be married on the 13th. (See Friday, the 13th; thirteen.)

phobophobia:
See phobias.

photographs:
See upside down pictures.

phrenology:
"The art" of character reading from the size and shape of the human skull. Franz J. Gall, M.D., the anatomist, developed this as a "science" basing his theory upon the view that the outer surface of the skull corresponded with the contours of the brain and that regions of the brain were correlated with character traits.

A high forehead is held to be a sign of leadership and a

reflective mind. Large eyes are the sign of benevolence and wonder. Wide skulls indicate pugnacity.

In America Dr. Charles Caldwell popularized the "science" in public platform lectures around the country in the second decade of the 19th century. For a quarter of a century he was the most eminent of American phrenologists. In 1832 Dr. Johann Spurzheim, collaborator with Dr. Gall, visited America and brought on a great revival of interest in phrenology. Even American physicians were "taken in" by him. Popular opinion, of course, was highly sympathetic and, for a time, phrenology was regarded as a "science." One could have his head "charted" for a fee of $5.00. Since that day phrenology has continued largely among circus and carnival entertainers with the usual quota of the credulous. See character reading.

physiognomy:
A "science" which is built upon the theory that body characteristics reveal mental characteristics. For example, the size of the head, face, eyebrows, etc. are indicative of a character type. This "science" was popular in the 16th century, forbidden by the English Parliament in 1743. Many superstitions have been built up on this basis. See chin and jaw.

picking blackberries:
See dreams.

picking up a glove:
See glove.

picking up a knife:
See knife.

picking up a pin:
See pin.

picking up scissors:
See scissors.

pictures:
See mirror; upside down pictures.

pierced ears:
See ears, pierced.

pigeons:
See athletes; birds.

pig-jowls:
Many people in the south of the United States hold the superstitious belief that the eating of pig-jowls and blackeyed peas on New Year's Day will bring good luck throughout the year.

pigs:
See black pig; fishermen; swine.

pillow and memory:
See memory.

pillow, books under:
See examinations.

pillow, extracted tooth under:
See tooth extraction.

pillow, hops in:
See hops in a pillow.

pillow, name under:
See marriage prospects.

pillow, piece of wedding cake under:
See wedding cake.

pillow, sifter under:
See fairy faith.

pin:
It is an omen of good luck to find a pin, particularly a safety pin.

See a pin and pick it up
All that day you will have luck
See a pin and let it lay
You'll have bad luck all that day.

On the contrary, there is the saying "Pick up a pin, pick up sorrow." "Pass up a pin, pass up a friend."

Black-headed pins must not be used when having a dress fitted; pins stuck in a wax image of a person brings pain to the latter.

A hairpin which becomes loose in the head is a sign of a sweetheart who is now in thoughts about you.

Pick up a pin with its head towards you. This insures having a ride soon (New England). See card playing; cures; knife; strangers.

pine bark:
See cures.

pine needles:
See coughs.

Pisces:
See astrology; birth stones.

pitchers (baseball):
See athletes.

planets:
See astrology.

plant:
If someone gives you a plant out of their garden and you thank him for it this will mean that the plant will not grow. See seeds.

plantain leaf:
See cures.

planting:
See cabbage; Good Friday; moon; potatoes, planting; seeds; spitting.

playing:
See fondling a cat.

playing cards:
See card playing.

plays:
See theatre.

plum bark:
See cures.

pocket:
See coat pocket; cures; horse chestnut; money.

pocket book:
See charm, lucky; coins.

pointing:
See moon, the new.

poison:
See aluminum cooking utensils; food, canned.

poison antidote:
See bedbugs.

poker:
See witches.

poles of the earth:
See getting out of bed.

Ponce de Leon:
See fountain of youth.

poppies:
See flowers.

pork:
See mole or wart.

pork, salt:
See cures.

pork, sliced:
See colds.

protruding chin:
See chin and jaw.

potatoes:
See cures; Good Friday; moon; onions; water lily roots.

potatoes, mashed:
See cures.

potatoes, planting:
When the sign of the Zodiac "is in the flower" all you get, when planting potatoes, will be blossoms and no potatoes. Gardening must follow the signs of the Zodiac.

Potatoes should be planted with the eyes up "so they can see to grow." (The fact is, however, that potatoes grow as well with eyes planted down.) See Good Friday.

pottery:
See breaking pottery; wedding anniversaries.

poultices:
See cures.

pouring cream in cup of coffee:
When cream is poured in a cup of coffee and bubbles appear: if the bubbles float away this is a sign you are going to lose money, if the bubbles float toward you this means you will receive money. See bubbles in a coffee cup.

poverty:
See birth; bread; mole or wart; spiders.

powder spilling:
This is supposed to bring on a quarrel with a friend. See theatre.

power:
See mesmerism; wand, magic.

power of the evil eye:
See evil eye.

practical nature:
See palmistry.

pranks:
See fairy faith.

prayers:
See yawning.

praying mantis:
An insect regarded by many as a symbol of holiness and therefore bad luck comes to him who kills it. If it seems to kneel down to him who observes it there will come a vision of an angel.

In the southern part of the United States it is called an agent of the devil. It should be left alone.

If a praying mantis alights on one's hand one will meet a distinguished person; if on the head one will shortly receive some great honor. If it injures one, one will lose a valued friend.

Its "holiness" rests on the suggestion arising from its observed posture which is that of clasped front legs.

preachers:
See ministers and bishops.

preachers and women:
Preachers and women aboard ship are considered by sailors to bring bad luck to a ship.

preaching to the fish:
Among the American Indians certain designated preachers, with powerful voices, preached to the fish during which time his fellows, sitting on the bank, would listen and ponder. It was believed that the fish would respond by seeking to be caught by the friendly rather than the hostile tribe.

Words spoken in full voice thus convey magic—an incantation.

prediction:
See hepatoscopy; prognostication.

prenatal influences:
It has been widely believed that emotional disturbances of an expectant mother (anger, fright, horror) may mark an unborn child by some injury or deformity.

This superstitious belief is discredited by modern medical knowledge. The only connection between mother and the unborn infant (outside the warmth and nourishment provided by the mother) is via the umbilical cord. This cord does not possess nerve fibers and hence such impressions are not transmitted.

Presidents' deaths:
See "fatal 20" superstition.

prevention of harm:
See looking into the eyes.

pricking:
See thumb pricking.

pride:
See palmistry; water lily roots.

primroses:
See flowers.

prize fighters:
See chin and jaw.

professors, college:
See memory.

prognostication:
See Christmas prognostication; hepatoscopy; prophecy; weather prognostication.

prognostics:
See dreams; ears, burning or ringing in the; omens; omens, bad; omens, good; strangers.

project, announcing beforehand:
See announcing a project beforehand.

prophecy:
See Bible divination; palmistry; phrenology; prognostication.

prosperity:
See financial prosperity; health; mistletoe; rice throwing; spider webs; teeth; wealth.

protection:
See birds; evil eye; jar of water with an immersed knife.

Proverbs, Book of:
See Bible divination.

prudence:
See palmistry.

Prysock, Arthur:
It is bad luck to this singer if he does not have a copy in his pocket of "Ave Maria." It was the first solo which he learned as a choir boy.

Pueblo tribes:
See snake dance.

pugnacity:
See phrenology.

pullets:
See hens.

pulling children's ears:
See ears.

pumpkins:
Pumpkins will breed worms in the stomach and cause itching. However, pumpkins are good for eye-sight (Maine).

Punxsutawney Club:
See ground hog.

purging of sins:
See death.

purple:
The color of royalty. It is the color of second mourning, a compromise between black and gay colors. See star-sapphire, purple; weather prognostication.

pyromania:
See moon, the new.

pyrophobia:
See phobias.

quail:
See weather prognostication.

quarrels:
See crime; dish rag; dreams; fences; hands crossing; knife; nose itching; powder spilling; washing; wiping on a towel.

quilt, new:
See dreams.

Quimby-ism:
"Dr." Phineas Parkhurst Quimby (d.1866), a blacksmith, mesmerist, born in New Hampshire and living in Maine, practiced faith cures. Sybil Wilbur in *The Life of Mary Baker Eddy* (1913) reports that Mary Baker Glover Patterson (who became the famous Mother Eddy of Christian Science) found in Quimby a means to a cure for her affliction of invalidism. (There is, of course, nothing superstitious about this.) Quimby's fame had spread throughout New England. His method was that of hypnotism (without religious connotation). (Another of Quimby's better known patients was Warren F. Evans, a Swedenborgian minister who "laid the foundations of the New Thought movement.")

Quimby-ism as a superstition lay not in Quimby's faith cures or his unrecognized hypnotic powers but in the bizarre ideas associated with his alleged occult powers. A forceful and undisciplined person (education meager and illiterate in spelling and punctuation, and yet shrewd) Quimby travelled with one Lucius Burkmer over whom he exerted strong hypnotic influence. When hypnotized Burkmer (or Burkman) claimed he could see into the bodies of persons (including Quimby's patients), penetrate into their condition and prescribe remedies. Testimonies of his strange powers include: "I have good reason to believe that he can discern the internal structure of an animal body and if there be anything morbid or defective therein detect and explain it." He was said to pass from point to point without passing through intermediate space, "from Belfast [Maine] to Washington or from the earth to the moon." (Dresser, *The Quimby Manuscripts*.)

Quimby interpreted Burkmer's powers those of thought-discernment and the cures in the patients' confidence. Quimby came to revise mesmerism with doctrines of his own. His diagnosis of bronchitis, for example, was the following: "You listen or eat this belief or wisdom [evidently that bronchitis is real] as you would eat your meals. It sets rather hard upon your stomach; this disturbs the error of your body and a cloud appears in the sky. . . . The elements of the body of your belief are shaken, earth is lit up by the fire of your error, the heat rises, the heaven or mind grows dark . . . the lightning of hot flashes shoot to all parts of the solar system of your belief. At last the winds or chills strike the earth or surface of the body, a cold clammy sensation passes over you. This changes the heat into a sort of watery substance which works its way into the channels and pores to the head and stomach." (*Quimby Manuscripts*, p. 118)

Disease is thus explained as a conglomerate mixture of physiology, psychology and metaphysics with mixed metaphors and undisciplined explanations! See mesmerism.

R

rabbit:

It is bad luck if a rabbit runs across one's path. If one returns and starts again this omen may be cancelled. Among certain American Negroes it is held that if a rabbit crosses from left to right the luck is good but if from right to left it portends something bad.

If a rabbit's fur is thick this is an omen of a hard winter, if thin, a mild one. See Easter egg.

rabbit's foot:

A rabbit's foot is a charm to bring good luck. (Carried as recently as December 1956 by the successful New Maid of Cotton, Helen Landon, in the cottonbelt beauty contest.) See charm, lucky; moon; theatre.

racial superstition:

The superiority of one "race" over against another is a long traditional belief. The Jews, for example, believed strongly in their own superiority (expressed in their conviction of being "chosen" people of God). Religious groups (national as well) carry on the notion of superiority in their traditions. Calvinism taught its own peculiar excellence, a plan of salvation of the elect; Catholicism has asserted its claim to the main highway of salvation. These claims, of course, are not racial but they belong to the whole emphasis of superiority comparable to racial superiority. The common fallacy lies in the tendency to be blind to values in other traditions.

As far as racial ideas of superiority are concerned, anthropologists claim that a superior race as such is a fiction.

(There may well be grades of "better and less" in cultures.) All humans are mongrel (mixtures of many bloods).

Negro blood is said to be different from white man's blood. (The fact is that the "blood of all races is almost identical" and blood transfusion is safe on the test of cross-matching rather than racial).

rain:
To walk outdoors during a rain while the sun is shining brings good luck.

"Preparation for rain scares it away." Hence, carry an umbrella.

See April showers; birds; bride; card playing; car wash; dog; Easter Sunday; headache; moon; snake dance; spiders; umbrella; weather prognostication.

rain barrel:
See iron water.

rainbow:
See weather prognostication.

rain water:
See eye trouble.

rake:
A rake carried with its teeth up during a harvest will foretell a wet harvest. See witches.

rappings:
These are allegedly spiritual manifestations—disclosures from spirits by means of coded noises through an appropriate medium.

A certain Almira Beazeley, a young lady of Providence, became an "artist" in communicating "revelations" by rappings, murdered her brother to fulfill a prediction and made confession in her trial that these rappings were of her own manipulations.

A wave of such rappings hit New York State during the

185

last century, Hydesville and later Rochester, particularly. The Weemans and the Fox sisters "experienced" slight knockings "at night in the bedroom" (1848).

Charles W. Ferguson in his *The Confusion of Tongues* (1928) says "Margaret [Fox], the older sister and the more capable of the two, repudiated her connexion with the movement [Spiritualism] entirely, told the world that it was humbuggery of the grossest sort, and, not content with this, gave a public performance in New York in 1888, during which she showed the audience that the mysterious rappings of the spirit were performed with her big toe and the big toe of her sister Kate." (p. 22.)

(It is a strange paradox that a spiritual interpretation of the world of reality should need to be undergirded by a claim to *physical* evidences!)

rats:
Rats leaving one house for another are said to bring bad luck to those who live in the house from which they have left and good luck to those whose house they have entered. Rats will not go through a soaped hole (New England). Catch a rat and paint it and let it run loose again. When other rats see this strange creature (painted rat) they will flee the area. (This happens not to be true.) See mouse traps and rat traps; ships; weather prognostication.

raw meat:
See meat eating.

Ray, Edward:
See athletes.

razor:
See moonshine.

reading gravestone epitaphs:
See gravestone epitaphs.

reaping:
See moon, the new.

receding chin:
See chin and jaw.

red:
See bulls see red; colors; corn; hex; peeling an apple; weather prognostication.

red head girls:
A "red head" is emotionally unstable and of terrible temper. An extreme superstition carries the rebuke that such a person "deserves to be burned as a witch."

A red-haired woman who comes too close to a cheese vat, tending it, will cause the curd of cheese to become "like loose sand" and therefore unfit to eat.

The appearance of a white horse will herald the appearance of a red-head girl. Conversely, the appearance of a red-head girl soon will be followed by the appearance of a white horse. (New England) See bees; horse(s); witches.

red meat:
See meat eating.

red pepper tea:
See cures.

red string:
A red string worn around the neck will ward off rheumatism. See rheumatism; string.

reflective mind:
See palmistry; phrenology; sneezing.

Regan, Ben:
See Anti-Superstition Society.

relief of pain:
See pain relief.

re-marriage:
See hair line.

remedies:
See cures.

remembering:
See ears; memory.

repentance:
See seeing one's shadow.

repetition:
See history.

repetition of events:
See fires follow fires.

restlessness:
See moonshine.

revelation:
See divination; magic crystal; rappings.

rheumatism:
See birds; cures; eel skin; growing pains; hops in a pillow; metallic tractors; red string; storm.

rhyme making:

"Make a rhyme without design
See your lover before bedtime."

rice pudding:
See almond.

rice throwing:
Rice, the symbol of health and prosperity, thrown at newly-weds is the charm to bless the marriage with many children.

riches:
See dreams; eyebrows; hair; mole; wealth.

ridding a house of ants:
This can be accomplished—so a Louisiana superstition says —by throwing coffee grounds under the steps to the kitchen; also, by taking some ants in a leaf to a neighbor's house (on the idea that others will follow).

Since ants will not cross a chalk mark, getting rid of ants involves only the use of chalk, drawing a circle around the area you want to protect (New England).

ride, going for a ride:
See journey; scratch on the back of the hand.

right ear:
See ears.

right eye:
If the right eye itches this is a sign that you are going to laugh. See nose itching.

right foot:
See getting out of bed.

right hand:
See clockwise; hand itching; handshaking; moon, the new; stirring the Christmas pudding; wine passing.

right hand pocket:
See money.

right side:
See birds; getting out of bed; squirrel.

right, stirring to the:
See soap.

right toe:
See toes.

ring:
See dactyliomancy; eye trouble; Hampton, Lionel; jewelry; pearl; wedding ring.

ringing or burning in the ear:
See ears, burning or ringing in the.

Roberts, Kenneth:
See dowser.

robin:
The appearance of a robin may mean the sign of a forthcoming fulfillment of a wish or it may mean death. See birds; thrush.

rock-crystal:
See magic crystal; wedding anniversaries.

rocking an empty chair:
It is bad luck to rock an empty chair (New England). See chair; empty seat.

rod:
See wand, magic.

rod, dowsing:
See dowsing rod.

Rogers, Will:
See clothes, old; knock on wood.

rolling eggs:
See Easter egg.

rolling over:
See horse(s).

Roodmas:
See witches.

Roosevelt, Franklin D.:
See "fatal 20" superstition.

rooster:
A rooster crowing on the doorstep is the sign of a stranger about to appear.

A rooster crowing in the midle of the night is an omen of bad news. The direction of the pointing of the rooster's head suggests the direction of the bad news. People have arisen at night to visit the roost to find out whence trouble is coming. See hens; omens, bad; weather prognostication.

roots:
See water lily roots.

rosy cheeks:
See bread crust.

ruby:
See birth stones; wedding anniversaries.

rum:
Rum poured on the head will insure against baldness and even make hair curly (Maine). See hair; sciatica.

running ears:
See ears, running.

running of the sap:
See wind, the.

rusty nail:
See stepping on a rusty nail.

S

Sabbath:
See Sunday.

Sabbath, witches':
See witches.

sadness:
See fortune telling; sorrow.

safety:
See incompletion; looking into the eyes.

safety pin:
See pin; sneezing.

sage tea:
See baldness.

Sagittarius:
See astrology; birth stones.

sailors:
A person or a thing which is held to cause bad luck on a voyage has been called a "Jonah." A small fish catch after a new person joins the crew makes him a Jonah.

It has been a common superstition among sailors that: it is unlucky to have an umbrella brought aboard a vessel; it is unlucky to drive nails on Sunday; if a bee or small bird lands on the ship, it is the sign of good luck but if a hawk or owl or crow alights on the rigging it is a sign of bad luck.

A horseshoe nailed to the mast protects against witches.

If one watches a ship out of sight it will never be seen again.

It is good to whistle for a breeze when the weather is calm; if the wind is to be fair it helps to stick a knife in the after side of the main mast.

Beware of a man coming aboard with a black valise. He is a Jonah.

It is lucky accidentally to drop a cake of ice overboard in preparation for a fishing expedition.

It is a sailor's traditional superstition that it is unlucky to set sail on a Friday but lucky to sail on Sunday:

Sunday sail, never fail
Friday sail, ill luck and gale.

See ears, pierced; mast, ship's; preachers and women; ships; warning of death; weather prognostication; whistling.

Saint Christopher:
Saint Christopher was a legendary martyr of the 3rd century who carried travellers across streams as his trade. One night he carried a child whose weight was too great for his own superlative strength and he was forced into the water. This child, says the legend, was Christ carrying the world in his hands. He became converted from his service to the Devil and began to serve the child even to martyrdom.

Christopher became the patron saint of ferrymen—and of travellers of every kind. The feast of Christopher is celebrated on July 25.

Many people today would not hazard a trip by car, boat, plane or any vehicle without the token-charm of St. Christopher as an assurance of a safe journey. See travelling.

Saint Dunstan:
See horseshoe.

Saint Germain:
See St. Germain.

Saint Joseph's Day:
See birds.

Saint Michael's Day:
See goose.

Saint Nicholas:
See Santa Claus.

Saint Patrick's Day:
See cabbage.

Saint Valentine's Day:
See marriage.

Salem incident:
See witches.

salesmen:
A salesman will, if he is superstitious, continue to wear the same necktie that he wore on his first sale—to the end of his trip—as a good luck charm. It may, in some instances, be the same suit of clothes. A forgotten order-book will be sent for to insure good luck, rather than to take chances on a new pad. A change of clothes or a bath may bring better luck to a salesman suffering from sales' failures.

Twirling a lucky coin in the left hand may bring the potential customer to the decision favorable to the salesman. A horseshoe in a trunk of samples is a charm.

salt, a plate of:
See death; moving into a new home.

salt carrying:
See moving into a new home.

salt fish:
Sun cured salt fish, a favorite article of diet of many New Englanders (Maine Islands), has issued in many folk ideas and customs. One superstition associated with salt fish was to the effect that if a "dream line" (strip in the center) is eaten before going to bed a girl or young man would see in a

vision the person who is to become her or his marital partner handing out a glass of water. See fish.

salt passing:
"Pass me salt, pass me sorrow."

salt spilling:
It is bad luck to spill salt. Throwing salt over the left shoulder will ward off bad luck.

See Friday, the 13th; moving into a new home; omens, bad.

salutation:
See waiters at tables.

San Juan Capistrano:
See birds.

San Juan's Day:
See birds.

Santa Claus:
Christmas as a modern carnival centers around a major superstition. Santa comes from the north pole (where he lives the year around) in his sleigh, dressed in red cap and jacket and enters the house through the chimney. He is a merry and fat individual full of chuckles. He has at his disposal gifts of whatever kind that could be wished for—nothing is too fabulous nor too trivial but what he can provide it. Children must be good and promise exemplary conduct to share in his generosity—but no child is ever passed by whatever the circumstances, if Santa has his will. Parents have access to him, smuggling the information he wants, to give all youngsters a rousing time. His reindeers which draw his overladen sleigh pass over the landscape unseen and yet their harness bells can be heard in the stillness of the night of Christmas eve anywhere. He prefers children to hang up their stockings—much, much too small receptacles—near the chim-

ney. He never complains of any irregularity of procedure, respecting the customs of each home.

Santa is the modern Saint Nicholas, a bishop in Asia Minor of the 4th century. Nicholas distributed gifts to the poor and sweets to children.

sap, running of the:
See wind, the.

sapphire:
See birth stones; wedding anniversaries.

sardonyx:
See birth stones.

sassafras:
The burning of sassafras brings bad luck (southern United States). See mole or wart.

Satan:
See devil; witches.

Saturday:
To start anything on Saturday is to begin something one will not live to see completed. See cutting finger nails; days of the week; dreams; fortune telling; incompletion; sneezing; moving into a new home.

Saturn:
See astrology; palmistry.

sauerkraut:
Made by older women sauerkraut will be good; made by young ones it will spoil.

saving money:
See money saving.

saving stamps:
See like brings like.

saying farewell:
See waving farewell.

scapulimancy:
Also called omoplatoscopy. Reading the future from the features of an animal's shoulder blade. (In England: reading the speal bone.)

scare-crows:
See birds.

scarlet:
The color of sinfulness. The devil is represented in scarlet color. See colors.

sceptre:
See wand, magic.

schism:
See musical instruments.

sciatica:
See cures.

scissors:
Never pick up scissors dropped to the floor. It is bad luck if you do. Ask someone else to pick them up if you wish to avoid the consequences. See strangers.

Scorpio:
See astrology; birth stones.

scratch on the back of the hand:
If a scratch occurs on the back of a hand and points toward the thumb—this is a sign that you are going for a ride. A long scratch means a long ride; a short scratch a short ride. And, "Nearer the thumb, Sooner it'll come." (New England)

screeching of an owl:
See omens, bad; owl.

sea hawks:
See birds.

seal of the United States:
See thirteen.

seamstress:
See sewing.

seasons:
See birds; birth; fruit stains; weather prognostication.

seat:
See empty seat.

sea witch of Billingsgate
See fairy faith.

second coming of Christ:
See shooting stars and comets.

seeds:
It brings bad luck to anyone who receives seeds and thanks the giver. (North Carolina) See fennel seed; garden seeds; grape seeds; meetin' seeds; moon; plant; planting.

seeing one's shadow:
A superstitious belief associated with the Hoshana Rabba of the Jewish calendar. This festival day is one of reprieve for those who have not repented during the season of repentance immediately preceding. If a person cannot see his shadow at nightfall on this day he is certain to die within the year.

To see one's shadow cast by the moon is considered by some to be an omen of bad luck.

seeing red:
See bulls see red.

self-restraint:
See chin and jaw.

September:
See birth stones; marriage.

seven:
For some seven is a lucky number, for others unlucky. To be the seventh child in a family is good luck. It is a sacred number in Jewish tradition: seven meaning completeness (on the seventh day God rested from his work of creation). The Old Testament abounds with sevens: seven years of plenty, seven of famine; the fall of Jericho involved the seventh day, seven priests, etc. See bridesmaid; corn; Easter Sunday; horsemen; lady bug; lottery; mirror; mistletoe; names.

sewing:
It is a sign of early death to the wearer of a garment which is stained by blood drawn from a finger pricked by a needle in sewing. A thimble lost while making a dress for a bride is a sign of good fortune for the bride. Sewing on the wrong side by mistake so that re-sewing is necessary is an omen of good luck. An all white dress in the making is a sure sign of good fortune.

A bride must not help sew her own wedding dress. This brings bad luck. A seamstress who tries on a bride's dress and wears it will herself become a bride. To sew a mourning dress for a young widow is the sign of an early marriage for the seamstress. It is bad luck for a wearer of a garment which has mistakenly been sewed by the wrong color thread.

Sewing on Sunday brings no harm providing a thimble is not used. Sewing on Sunday will cause the Devil to take the stitches out at night (a Southern superstition). "Sew on Sunday, rip up stitches on Monday." See dress material.

shadow:
See seeing one's shadow; ground hog.

Shakespeare, quoting from:
See theatre.

shaking hands:
See handshaking.

shamrock:
The shamrock plant is held by those of Irish descent as a charm of good luck. Their ancestors exchanged the shamrock at the time of betrothal (similar to the modern practice of the gift of engagement rings or pins). Irish soldiers carried shamrocks as good luck charms when they undertook the risks of battle.

sharks:
Sharks following a ship is an ominous sign.

sheep:
It is considered good luck to meet a flock of sheep. See weather prognostication.

shelling peas:
See nine.

shining of the sun:
See rain; Wednesday.

ship names:
See names.

ships:
Watch rats before putting to sea. If they leave, the ship will be lost. See fishermen; mast, ship's; ocean liners; phantom ship; preachers and women; sailors; sharks; whistling.

shirts:
It is considered bad luck to wear shirts that have buttons. Duke Ellington, for example, insists on pull-over shirts made especially for him. "I feel that button shirts hold me in. They give me that repressed feeling." On one occasion he delayed a London concert appearance for 35 minutes while his valets sought a slip-over shirt. He holds it to be bad luck to wear button shirts. See undershirt.

200

shivering:

Among Southern mountaineers shivering means that some-one is walking over the spot of your grave. Among Negroes it means being in love.

shoe laces:

If a shoe lace is untied it is a sign that someone is thinking or talking about you.

shoes:

Frank Craven, the actor, insisted that his shoes never be placed on a shelf higher than his head, to avoid bad luck.

Band leader Dizzy Gillespie, the bebop king, remembered his grandmother's superstition (from South Carolina geechie folk lore): never to put shoes on a shelf. A woman who put her shoes on a shelf had been hit by their fall and later went crazy. His wife, Lorraine, absentmindedly put three new pairs of his expensive shoes on a shelf. When Dizzy returned and found them he promptly threw all of them into the furnace. This incident, he relates, almost broke up his home.

It is a sign of bad luck to walk with only one shoe (or slipper). It may be a sign of death.

Throwing shoes or tying shoes to going-away baggage or means of transportation of a bride and groom is an old custom (e.g. Scottish) which is supposed to be a symbol of good luck as well as a "fruitful" marriage. A shoe of the bride thrown among wedding guests is an old Scandinavian custom.

The shoe as a symbol of fertility is perhaps implied in the Mother Goose rhyme:

"There was an old woman who lived in a shoe
She had so many children she didn't know what to do."

See cramps; cutting finger nails; dressing; shoes' squeak; theatre.

201

shoes' squeak:
This broadcasts the information that they are not paid for.
See theatre.

shooting stars and comets:
If a shooting star (or a meteor) sweeps visibly across the
sky good luck will come your way, especially if you make
a wish for money. A sick person beholding such a phenomenon will be certain to be restored to health within thirty days.
On a voyage a shooting star is the sign of a successful trip.
Lovers who make a wish together while seeing a shooting
star will find this to be an omen of a fulfilled wish for good
health, wealth and prosperity.

Comets are omens of disaster. In medieval times Christian
Catholics saw in a comet the signal of the imminent second
coming of Christ. The end of the present order is associated
with the appearance of comets. A comet in the sky instills
fear and induces prayers for protection. Wars, pestilence and
famines are the usual predictions associated with them. No
one will do any business of importance during a comet's visi-
tation.

Children born under a comet's appearance in the sky will
suffer misfortune and may be expected to die suddenly. See
stars.

shoulder blades:
See scapulimancy.

showers:
See rain.

sick room:
See feathers.

sick, the:
See cures; death; dreams; dying; fondling a cat; illness;
nail cutting; shooting stars and comets; sneezing; warning of
death.

sidewalks:
See stepping on a crack.

sieve:
See coscinomancy.

sifter under a pillow:
See fairy faith.

sight:
See eyes.

sign of the cross:
See cross, sign of; friends.

signs:
See death, signs of approaching; left eye; omens; omens, bad; omens, good; personality characteristics; right eye; shoe laces; tongue; visitors coming.

silk:
See wedding anniversaries.

silliness:
See colors.

silver:
See mast, ship's; wedding anniversaries.

silver coins, shaking:
See moon, the new.

simpleton:
See lice.

sing before breakfast:

"If you sing before seven,
you'll cry before eleven."

"If you sing before you eat
you'll cry before you sleep."

See getting out of bed.

203

singing:
If one happens to sing while bathing this is a sign of good luck. See card playing; children.

singing tea-kettle:
See tea-kettle.

sinister:
See getting out of bed.

sins, purging of:
See purging of sins; scarlet.

sitting on table:
See table sitting.

six:
See katydid.

skull:
See phrenology; voodoo.

skunks:
See cures; weather prognostication.

sky:
See thunder.

sky colors:
See weather prognostication.

sleep:
Older people need less sleep than younger. (Behold their habit of early rising!)

This superstitious error, once common, is challenged by the best medical authorities of today. The fact is, older people need more rest than young and usually get it in cat naps.

sleeping:
See examinations; grinding of teeth; moon; moonshine; sing before breakfast; strange bed; young people.

sleeping on a bear skin:
See cures.

sleep walking:
An old belief has been widely held that a sleepwalker should never be awakened quickly, else he may die.

sleepy:
Being sleepy after dinner dishes means that company is coming.

slip under a lady's dress:
If her slip hangs longer than her dress this is a sign that her father loves her more than does her mother.

A slip or undergarment that is put on inside out should not be changed but worn as it is. To change is to invite bad luck.

slipping of soap:
See soap.

small ears:
See ears, small.

smart weed:
See colds.

smell:
See odor.

smile:
See theatre.

Smithsonian Institution:
See Hope diamond.

smoke:
See capnomancy.

smoking:
Boys are told that smoking stunts growth. (No evidence— a plain superstition.) See cigarette lighting.

snake:
See dreams; horse-hair; omens, bad.

snake ball:
See cures.

snake bite:
See cures.

snake dance:
The Pueblo tribes evolved elaborate ceremonial rites—
the snake dance—to induce the spirits to give them rain.

snakes travel in pairs:
This belief is unfounded. Usually snakes inhabit a vicinity
but do not move about in pairs. Thus the killing of a snake
is said to bring on the revenge of its "partner" is a superstition (not only in the idea of alleged "pairs" but in the attributing of a person's own reactions to snakes. See pathetic fallacy.

snapping a twig or match:
See snapping the fingers.

snapping the fingers:
This gesture, like the snapping of a twig or match in two,
is supposed to bring on a "lucky break." It is thought that the
origin of this performance is an outgrowth of noise making
to frighten the evil spirits away.

sneezing:
It is an omen of good luck if one sneezes three times.

It is a sure sign of an approaching wedding if one sneezes
before getting up on Sunday morning.

It is good luck to say "God bless you" when a baby
sneezes.

If a sick person sneezes this is a sign that he will get well.

Sneezing associated with thinking is the sign that what he
thinks will come true.

A bride or groom better not sneeze. It is a sign of bad luck. Sneezing has been associated with days of the week:

"Sneeze on Monday, sneeze for danger;
Sneeze on Tuesday, kiss a stranger;
Sneeze on Wednesday, sneeze for a letter;
Sneeze on Thursday, something better;
Sneeze on Friday, sneeze for sorrow;
Sneeze on Saturday, your sweetheart to morrow;
Sneeze on Sunday, your safety seek,
Or the devil will have you all the week."

Another rhyme has another version:

Sneeze on Monday, sneeze for health;
Sneeze on Tuesday, sneeze for wealth;
Sneeze on Wednesday, the best of all;
Sneeze on Thursday, sneeze for losses;
Sneeze on Friday, sneeze for crosses;
Sneeze on Saturday, no luck at all;
Sneeze on Sunday, the bad man will be with you all next week." (Southern United States)

An ancient superstition held that a first sneeze prompted death.

Sneezing before breakfast is a sign that company is coming.

It is an old tradition that when one sneezes someone should call out some magical formula, e.g., "God bless you" or "Gesundheit" (Good Health). A sneeze may be regarded as a good omen: the symbol of the entrance into the body of a good spirit, probably that of an ancestor. A sneeze is also an unfavorable omen: the symbol of a possession of an evil spirit.

See getting out of bed.

207

snipe flies:
See flies.

snow:
See moon; washing hair; weather prognostication.

snow flakes:
See storm.

snow storm:
See marriage; storm.

soap:
Among the North Carolina legends the making of soap has acquired specific ideas: soap will not set unless made on the full moon. The increase of the moon will help thicken it. If a woman makes soap and the man stirs it will turn out well; but if another woman stirs it will turn out ill. Soap should be stirred only to the right. Bad luck will come if the stirring is not sunwise.

Hold soap securely lest it slip away. If it does slip from the hand so will good fortune.

See moon; rats; theatre.

sock, woolen:
See colds.

sore on the tip of tongue:
See tongue.

sore throat:
See cures.

sores, mouth:
See cures.

sorrow:
See crows; fortune telling; pin; salt passing; sneezing; sweeping dust; tears.

"soul mate"
See love at first sight.

sour:
See fortune telling.

south:
See north-south.

south-paw pitcher:
See athletes.

south wind:
See wind.

speaking, someone speaking of you:
See ears, burning or ringing in the; shoe laces.

speaking ill of:
See lip itching.

speculation:
See April Fool's Day; February 29; money.

spell:
See charm; evil eye; feathers; forgetting; hand itching; harvest; hex; jar of water with an immersed knife; luck, bad; mirror; stumbling on a threshold; voodoo.

spendthrift:
See thumbs.

spider bites:
See cures.

spider webs:
Spider webs in a house are a sign of prosperity (except to many Louisiana natives).

spiders:
To kill a spider is to bring rain or poverty. If a spider approaches this is a sign of a letter that is coming. If a spider is seen on one's clothing this is an omen that one will be getting new clothes. Cobwebs in the grass mean rain before

nightfall; in the house they are bad omens. A spider in a shell hung around the neck is good for the health.

"If you want to live and thrive
Let the spider run alive" (Maine).

See omens, bad.

spike-root tea:
See cures.

spilling powder:
See powder spilling.

spilling salt:
See salt spilling.

spilling sugar:
See sugar spilling.

spilling wine:
See toasting.

spinster:
See bachelor; bread; mirror.

spiritism:
See mesmerism.

spirits:
See birds; death; evil spirits; fairy faith; good spirits; hair; magic crystal; mirror; rappings; snake dance; sneezing; St. Germain; witches.

spiritualism:
See rappings.

spiritual life:
See spiritual vibrations.

spiritual vibrations:
It is a doctrine of certain religious cults (from India to

America) that people "are simply bundles of vibrating action" and by stepping these up great visions may be had. An "electro-body," the antithesis of the "physical body" (G. W. Ballard of Southern California) is to be attained by proper dedication to the spiritual life. See St. Germain.

spit in the hat:
See athletes.

spitting:
The superstition widely persists that spitting on the bait gives good luck to the fisherman; spitting on the hands also forebodes good; spitting into the left palm and slapping it with the right (using index finger), observing the splash, will give the direction wherein a lost article may be found (boys say: "Spit, spat, where is the ball at?" or, "Spit, spat spo, where did it go?"); spitting in the hole where a bush is to be planted is a ritual of good luck.
See athletes; horse(s); horsemen.

spoon:
See knife.

sports:
See athletes.

spring:
See birds; Easter day; weather prognostication.

spring delayed:
See ground hog.

spring tonic:
A traditionally American home remedy has been the mixture of sulphur and molasses taken in the spring to purify the blood.
See cures; Kickapoo Indian Sagwaw.

Spurzheim, Johann:
See phrenology.

squeaky shoes:
See shoes' squeak; theatre.

squirrel:
If a squirrel crosses your path it is a sign of good luck if it crosses to the right but bad luck if it crosses to the left in front of you (New England).

St.:
See under saint.

staff:
See wand, magic.

stage:
See actors and actresses; peacock; theatre; whistling back stage.

stains:
See fruit stains.

Stallings, George:
See athletes.

stamps:
See like brings like.

starching:
See ironing.

star falling:
Make a wish when a star falls and the wish will come true.

star, first:
The first star seen at night after leaving the house provides the occasion of a wish which promises fulfilment.

staring:
See evil eye.

star-ruby:
See wedding anniversaries.

212

stars:
See astrology; nine; shooting stars and comets; talisman; weather prognostication.

star sapphire, blue:
See wedding anniversaries.

star-sapphire, gray:
See wedding anniversaries.

star-sapphire, purple:
See wedding anniversaries.

start something:
See Friday; Saturday.

starting on a journey:
If the first object you encounter on starting on a journey is a woman or a cat this is a sign that bad luck will befall before your return. If the woman is bare foot—beware of severe bad luck. Best it is, then, to return and postpone the journey for another day. Do not place your left arm in your coat or jacket first for such procedure brings bad luck (New England).

steak:
See cures.

stealing:
See mole or wart.

steel plates:
See mesmerism.

steel workers:
Steel workers who walk bridges or climb girders give an extra twist to their suspenders or overall straps before they ascend to their hazardous work. This is for good luck. (There is more than a superstition involved here. A twisted suspender like a knotted string is a reminder to be careful.)

stepping into a house:

Placing the left foot first when entering a house is to bring bad luck.

See groom.

stepping on a crack:

As children many of us remember the chant: "Step on a crack and break your mother's back."

Bad luck is supposed to befall the person who steps on cracks in the sidewalk or between spaces of flagstone block walks.

See omens, bad.

stepping on a rusty nail:

"What did you do when you stepped on a rusty nail?" the Pennsylvania farmer was asked. "I pulled him out. I greased him good and I laid him away where he don't get wet," was the reply. "But what did you do for the wound?", he was asked again. "My wife, she got a lily leaf out of the whiskey bottle and laid it in the wound" was the reply. A case (in the first instance) of vicarious healing?

stepping on graves:

Always step over, or better, walk around graves. Walking on graves will bring bad luck.

St. Germain:

A medium popularly employed to communicate with invisible spirits. American Indians refer to St. Germain (Wisconsin), some carrying this as a family name. Mr. G. W. Ballard, founder of a popular religious cult, claimed contact with the oft-reincarnated St. Germain one night in Honolulu and "felt his thoughts go back to the students in America." His first major contact with St. Germain was on Mt. Shasta in whose presence he felt "so puny and tiny." "If your own vibrations were stepped up you might see St. Germain here today" he said to his followers (as reported in *The Chicago Tribune*, October 12, 1938).

See spiritual vibrations.

stinginess:
See ears, small.

stinging of bees:
See bees.

stirring:
See clockwise; soap.

stirring the Christmas pudding:
To have good luck stir with the right hand and from left to right.
See clockwise.

stockings:
If stockings are put on inadvertently wrong side out this is an omen of good luck.
See black stocking; dressing.

stomach disturbances:
See cures; pumpkins.

stones:
See birth stones; cures; talisman; voodoo; wedding anniversaries.

stork:
See birds.

storm:
If it storms on the first Sunday in the month you may expect storms on succeeding Sundays of the same month.
The wind whistling about the house is a sign of a storm.
Water boiling out of a kettle is a sign of a coming storm.
A cloud growing larger means a storm.

Snow flakes of a small size signal a long storm.

If a storm clears at night-fall look for another soon.

Rheumatism in the bones is prophetic of a storm brewing (probably in forty-eight hours). (New England)

See marriage; moon; weather prognostication; wedding day.

strange bed:

For the first time that you sleep in a strange bed you should name the four posts of the bed after your prospective bride or groom. In your dream the person who comes to mind will be the one of the four whom you will marry (New England).

Sleeping in a strange bed and dreaming portend a dream coming true.

See bed.

strangers:

A belief that a stranger is coming if a brand falls in the corner and remains upright; or, if a pin, needle, fork or a pair of scissors falls with point downward and sticks; or the peculiar appearance in the wick of a burning candle.

See guests; rooster; sneezing; visitors coming.

string:

See cramps; cures; red string; steel workers.

stroke, pain of:

See cures.

strong feeling:

See iron water.

stubbing the toes:

See toes.

stubby fingers:

See biting nails.

216

stumbling:
It is a sign of bad luck if one trips or stumbles at the beginning of the day.

Stumbling is generally a sign of tragedy. Recognized by such ancients as Pliny and Cicero.

stumbling on a threshold:
When setting out on an errand or journey, to stumble on the threshold is an omen of bad fortune ahead. One must return and begin again to break the spell. Highlander Scots were particularly sensitive to this superstition.

stunting growth:
See smoking.

stutter:
See tickling babies.

stye in the eye:
See eye trouble; flowers; wedding ring.

styles:
See jewelry.

success:
See birds; luck, good; palmistry; planting.

sucking thumbs:
See thumbs.

sugar:
See cane sugar.

sugar spilling:
Spilling sugar is far worse in its result for bad luck than the spilling of salt. It is worse since the ill fortune that follows cannot be overcome by dusting of a few grams across the shoulder. (A superstition listed among those compiled by the Agricultural Extension Service of the University of Florida.)

suggestion:
See voodoo.

217

suicide:
See bachelor; card playing.

sulphur:
See candle; cures; spring tonic.

sumac:
See cures.

summer:
See birds; birth.

sun:
See birth; Good Friday; shining of the sun; sunstroke; weather prognostication.

sun bathing:
See hair.

Sunday:
See crickets; cutting finger nails; dreams; Easter Sunday; fortune telling; hens; marriage; Sabbath, witches'; sailors; sewing; sneezing; storm.

sunshine:
See Christmas prognostication; Wednesday.

sunstroke:
White people, it is held, are more susceptible to sunstroke than the dark skinned. (A superstition nursed probably on the feeling of delicacy and superiority? This belief was dethroned in World War II when armies of white men, helmetless, withstood the rigors as well as others under the tropical sun.)

sun-wise:
See clockwise; soap.

superiority of races:
See racial superstition.

218

superstitions:
See Anti-Superstition Society.

surprise money:
See bubbles in a coffee cup.

swallowing:
See lilac.

swallows:
See birds; weather prognostication.

sweating:
See horse(s).

sweeping dust:
A common superstition is to the effect that in sweeping dust out of a house one is sweeping away good luck. Sweeping toward the center of the room and carrying the dust out by a bucket or pan will not bring on misfortune.

Sweeping has other associations: it is unlucky: to sweep after dark, to sweep dirt out on Friday or on Christmas day or New Year's.

"Sweep after dark
Sweep sorrow in your heart" (Maine).

sweetheart:
See dish rag; hem of a dress; love life; sneezing.

swine:
See pig-jowls; weather prognostication.

swollen joints:
See cures.

T

table:
See card playing; empty seat; hands crossing; salt passing; thirteen; waiters at tables; wine passing.

table sitting:
A sure sign of an approaching wedding is the circumstance of sitting upon a table. It is also a sign of a wish to get married.

table waiters:
See waiters at tables.

taking the last piece:
See bread.

talent:
It is becoming the fashion (a superstition?) to say that a person is born with such-and-such a talent or genius (without due regard for environmental influences, developing interests drawn from environment and hard work). Perhaps the factor of inborn talent is neglible as compared with the myriad of conditioning factors that impress upon a growing individual. See fruit trees, grafting; memory.

talisman:
This word is derived from the Arabic "tilsam," a magical image. It is a kind of charm, consisting of a figure engraved on stone, parchment or metal. It brings good luck by its alleged protective power to fence off evils. It is a form of amulet. Its original association lay with the stars (ancients). See amulets; carrying a holy book; charm, lucky.

talking, someone talking about you:
See burning a hole in a dress; ears, burning or ringing in the; lip itching; shoe laces.

tall:
See grow tall.

tansy tea:
See colds.

taphephobia:
See phobias.

tapping of beetles:
See beetles (wood boring).

Taurus:
See astrology; birth stones.

tea:
See colds; cures; pennyroyal tea; sage tea.

tea-kettle:
A "singing" tea-kettle is a sign of contentment in the home.

tea leaves:
One sign of approaching company is the floating of tea leaves in a vessel containing them.

tea-pot:
Allowing the lid of a tea-pot to stand open will bring a guest to tea.

tears:
See bride's first kiss; finding a handkerchief; pearl.

teeth:
Teeth wide apart indicate prosperity and happiness.
Front teeth set far apart show that the person will be a wanderer (New England). See beads and teeth; cures; grinding of teeth; tooth-ache; tooth extraction; tooth decay.

221

teeth of a wolf:
See cures.

teething:
See beads and teeth.

telling a fortune:
See fortune telling.

telling a lie:
See lie telling.

temper:
See bad temper; personality characteristics.

tenderness:
See palmistry.

Thales:
See memory.

thanatophobia:
See phobias.

thanks:
See plant; seeds.

theatre:
Some theatres regarded by actors as unlucky spots for performances are given other names to remove the "jinx." The results are said to be excellent (by such name changing).

There are many theatre superstitions: never whistle in the dressing-room; never open an umbrella on the stage; never use yellow curtains; on May 10th never quote from Shakespeare (particularly Macbeth) except during a regular performance. (This superstition probably dates back to a riot which occurred during a performance about 1849.)

If a cat walks across the stage at rehearsal this is an ill omen. (William Gillette, the actor, defied this superstition by keeping cats. At the Knickerbocker Theatre Lester, a black

222

and white cat was kept and used for good luck. This unknown cat wandered upon the stage at the opening night of
"Listen, Lester" and the play became a hit. Lester was there-
after the assurance of success.)

It is considered an invitation to bad luck to change a costume worn at a first play which brought success. It is good
luck to continue the wearing of the same costume even though
it becomes threadbare.

To repeat at rehearsals the last line of a play brings bad
luck. It is a bad omen to turn the handle of the wrong door
of a manager's or play-broker's office. Better then to return
home and start afresh on another day.

A drop curtain which forms a loop is a bad omen. Wigs
are considered lucky. Squeaky shoes are good omens. Kicking
off shoes brings good luck if they alight on their soles; if,
however, they fall on their sides this is a bad omen. A costume
snagged in the scenery upon entrance to the stage forebodes
bad luck; it is better then to make a new entrance. Peepholes
in the center of the stage curtain are permissible but off to
one side such peepholes foretell trouble.

Theatre managers have their characteristic superstitions: if
the first purchaser of seats for a performance is an elderly
person this means a "long run." However, if the first purchaser is young, the "run" will be short. A torn paper money
is a sign of bad fortune. Money of a large sum which calls for
change is a good omen. An usher seating a person in a seat
marked "thirteen" or its multiple will consider this an omen
of bad luck. A tip for a program is a good omen received
from a gentleman, a bad omen received from a lady. The
first tip of the season demands a brisk rubbing on the leg of
the trousers and then kept in the pocket for good luck. A
smile from an actor is good luck, especially from across the
footlights.

If a woman faints in the theatre or a death occurs in the
same place—these are bad omens for the play.

Artificial flowers are to be preferred over real flowers in

plays. (Fallen petals are potential dangers of possible falling of performers.) It is also bad luck to leave soap in a hotel or other places while on tour.

Chorus girls will dance on spilled powder to bring luck. A hare's foot is a charm for success. A fall on the stage is a sign of a long professional engagement.

Knitting on a stage by actresses is taboo. Winding a piece of discovered cotton around a finger without breaking will reveal a forthcoming contract with a theatrical management, his initial suggested by the number of turns involved in completing the winding. Three times equals the letter C, the name perhaps of a Noel Coward show.

Theatrical people are extraordinarily superstitious. It is said of them that were there no superstitions they would invent some.

Broadway dancers, since 1949, now speak of the musical "Gentlemen Prefer Blondes" as the beginning of a curse to add to the list of superstitions. A dancer by the name of Florence Baun owned a white satin cloak ornamented with a marabou collar. Wrapped in this garment she sensed a curse, noting that the wearing of the garment coincided with adverse comments of her performance. She gave the garment to a Mr. William Bradley who called it the "Gypsy Robe." He, in turn, passed it on to Stanley Simmons, a dancer in "Out of This World" commenting that a curse of the gypsies would follow unless he passed the robe on to another show. Gypsy Robe has thus been handed to someone associated with a new Broadway musical. It comes as a "surprise package" on opening night. Nancy Lynch, a dancer in "My Fair Lady" found the cloak in a whiskey carton in her dressing room. It had been passed on to her by Donald Weissmuller of "Pipe Dream." Miss Lynch passed it on to David Popwell of "Mr. Wonderful" and he plans (1956) to divest himself of this property in the accustomed manner.

The Gypsy Robe is embellished with some mementos from each musical. It has gold ankle bracelets from "The King and

I," a cigarette holder from "The Vamp," violets from "My Fair Lady," panties from "Can Can," a stuffed bird from "Fanny," sea shells from "Pipe Dream," pink tights from "The Girl in Pink Tights" and stockings from "Silk Stockings." It now weighs twenty five pounds. See actors and actresses; birds; Craven, Frank; Jolson, Al; peacock; shoes; thirteen.

thief:
See nail cutting.

thimble:
See sewing.

thinking person:
See chin and jaw.

thinking, someone thinking of you:
See shoe laces.

thirteen:
The number thirteen has been commonly considered unlucky. For example: never thirteen at a meal nor living in the same house.

Thirteen, however, has been considered by some to be a lucky number. Richard Wagner favored it. There are thirteen letters in his name; he was born in 1813; he composed thirteen operas. Ziegfeld considered it lucky. He preferred to sail on the 13th and would prefer to open a new show on the 13th. Woodrow Wilson favored it. On an occasion he was entertained at a dinner with thirteen guests. In spite of protests he announced that thirteen was a lucky number. (There are those who think that this and his Thirteen Points [reduced from Fourteen] contributed to his bad luck.)

On the seal of the United States there are thirteen stars and thirteen bars; an eagle with thirteen tail feathers holding thirteen darts; there are thirteen olives and the motto *E Pluribus Unum* has thirteen letters.

See Anti-Superstition Society; Friday, the 13th; hens; horsemen; phobias; theatre; triskaidekaphobia; wedding anniversaries.

thirty-nine:
See wedding anniversaries.

thistle root:
See cures.

thread:
See sewing.

three:
The number three has had lucky connotations. For Europeans it has been a mystic number in religion and medicine. The idea of Trinity implies completeness, fulfillment. Three connotes completeness as e.g., three strikes make an out, three outs make an inning. Three times is the final number for a person to come up before drowning.

Three may have unlucky significance, e.g., three people making up a bed foretells illness to one of them. Again, the old saying "Good or bad things come in threes," that is, with two good or bad events comes soon a third. See accidents; cigarette lighting; coughs; crows; dreams; Easter Day; fires follow fires; lottery; love life; marriage prospects; nutmegs; sneezing; thrice; wedding ring.

threshold:
See groom; stumbling on a threshold.

threshold, crossing:
See Kitt, Eartha; New Year.

thrice:
See card playing; sneezing; three.

thrift, lack of:
See finger nails.

226

throat:
See fish-bone; sore throat.

throwing coins:
See coins; mast, ship's.

throwing rice:
See rice throwing.

throwing salt:
See salt spilling.

thrush:
Generally known in America as the robin. See robin; weather prognostication.

thumb itching:
This signifies the coming of visitors. See guests; hand itching.

thumb pricking:
A sign of thumb pricking is that something bad is turning up.

"By the pricking of my thumb
Something evil this way comes" (Maine).

thumbs:
A thumb turned back is a sign of inability to save money.
If a baby sucks its thumb it will grow up to be hideous. See friends; scratch on the back of the hand.

thunder:
If it thunders and the sky is cloudless this is a sign of good luck.
Thunder after midnight means that it will be lowery on the day following (New England). See milk; weather prognostication.

thunderstorm:
Lightning will not strike during a thunderstorm if one gets himself a feather bed. (Southern United States) See marriage.

Thursday:
See cutting finger nails; days of the week; sneezing; fortune telling.

Tibuta, the witch:
See witches.

tickets:
See lottery.

tickling babies:
Tickling babies will cause them to stutter when they grow up.

tide:
See warning of death; weather prognostication.

tin:
See wedding anniversaries.

tipping:
See theatre; waiters at tables.

toads:
It is bad luck to kill a toad. See mole or wart; weather prognostication.

toasting:
To toast a friend is an ancient custom. One theory of its origin is that a piece of toast was dropped in the wine and the morsel became the symbol of the drinking to each other's health. Good health is the wish of toasting. To break a glass while engaged in toasting is an omen of bad luck. To spill wine while toasting is a sign of good luck. See wine passing.

228

toes:
Stubbing one's right toes is good luck but stubbing the left toes is bad. See fish-bone.

tokens of good luck:
People carry tokens with them for good luck. A metal disc in a pocket brings luck to a golfer. See birth stones; charm, lucky; luck, good; Saint Christopher; talisman; wedding anniversaries.

tongue:
A sore on the tip of the tongue is a sign that you told a lie (New England). See ears, burning or ringing in the.

tonic:
See moon.

tools:
See grave.

tooth-ache:
See cures.

tooth decay:
People hold that a clean tooth never decays. But much more is involved than cleanliness of the surface of teeth to healthy teeth.

tooth extraction:
Placing an extracted tooth under a pillow at night will bring good luck the following day. (Many parents assuage their child's pain and remembrance of an extraction by the promise of a visit by the fairy during the night replacing the tooth with a welcome present.) See teeth.

topaz:
See birth stones; friends; wedding anniversaries.

topaz-quartz:
See birth stones; wedding anniversaries.

tornadoes:
See atomic bomb tests.

touch wood:
See boasting; knock on wood.

tourmaline:
See birth stones.

towel:
See wiping on a towel.

tractors:
See metallic tractors.

tragedy:
See birds; dreams; fires follow fires; luck, bad; trouble.

traits of character:
See character reading; palmistry.

traps:
See mouse traps and rat traps.

travelling:
It is bad luck to travel on Monday but good luck to travel on Tuesday.

It is bad luck to take a trip immediately after hearing about the death of a friend. See Friday; Friday, the 13th; Saint Christopher; shooting stars and comets; yellow.

travelling salesmen:
See salesmen.

tree:
See fruit tree.

trip:
See journey; travelling.

tripping:
See stumbling.

triskaidekaphobia:
See Friday, the 13th; phobias.

trouble:
See dreams; eyebrows; luck, bad; rooster; tragedy.

trousseau:
It is unlucky to try on any wedding garments before the wedding day. See bride.

trunk:
See baggage.

trunk, empty:
John Cumberland, the actor, was very superstitious about sitting down on an empty trunk—an omen of bad luck.

trust and mistrust:
See eyes, green.

tuberculosis:
See dogs' fat.

Tuesday:
See cutting finger nails; days of the week; fortune telling; sneezing; travelling.

turkey:
See birds.

turning over in bed:
It is bad luck (New England superstition) to turn over in bed. The story is told of two men (who held this view) who, when they slept together, would wake up at midnight and each got out on his side of the bed and walked around the foot and then exchanged places in bed. Thus they found new positions without turning.

turnip-root:
See cures.

turnips:
See July 25.

turquoise:
See birth stones.

turtle dove:
See birds.

turtle shell ashes:
See cures.

twelve:
See lottery.

twenty:
See "fatal 20" superstition.

twenty-six:
See wedding anniversaries.

two:
See crows.

two dollar bills:
See money.

U

ugly:
See grow up hideous.

ulcers:
See cures.

umbrella:
Carrying an umbrella will ward off rainy weather. Do not open an umbrella in the house or it will bring bad luck. See lending; rain; sailors; theatre.

undergarment:
See slip under a lady's dress.

undershirt:
See athletes.

unhappiness:
See bride.

United States Naval Academy:
See coins.

United States Presidents:
See "fatal 20" superstition.

United States seal:
See thirteen.

unlucky:
See luck, bad.

unlucky at cards, lucky in love:
See card playing.

233

untied shoe laces:
   See shoe laces.

upside down:
   See clothing, putting on.

upside down pictures:
   To turn a picture upside down is to bring bad luck to the person or place which is the subject of the picture. An older superstition held that an upside down photograph or a picture turned to the wall was an invitation to lurking evil spirits to work their evil ways upon the subject.

usher:
   See theatre.

utensils, cooking:
   See aluminum cooking utensils.

V

valise:
See baggage; black valise.

valley:
See oil.

vans:
See moving into a new home.

Vaughan, Sarah:
In every performance she included the song "Tenderly" for good luck.

vehicle:
See fortune telling.

veil:
See birth with a veil.

velvet ant:
See wasp.

Venus:
See astrology.

vexation:
See nose itching.

vibrations, spiritual:
See spiritual vibrations.

vicarious healing:
See stepping on a rusty nail.

viciousness:
See chin and jaw.

victory:
See birds.

vinegar:
See mole or wart.

vines:
See moon.

Virgo:
See astrology; birth stones.

virtue:
See birds.

vision:
See evil eye; eyes; praying mantis; spiritual vibrations.

visionary person:
See palmistry.

visiting on Monday:
It is a sign that if you go out on a Monday you will be visiting out every day of that week (New England).

visitors coming:
See birds; cat washing its face; guests; knife; leaving a house; New Year; nose itching; rooster; sneezing; strangers; tea leaves; thumb itching.

vocation:
See Bible divination.

voodoo:
Throughout the world, including this country, many people believe in and practice voodoo, the power of hexing or casting spells. Generally surrounded by secrecy and expressed in complex rituals, victims are held under a power which overcomes their will. It is a form of suggestion. A hex itself can be un-hexed.

The Rev. Oliver, North Carolina Negro, an "authority" on

voodoo, speaks of a "spell" as containing the mind and a "hex" as a result of fear. Three kinds of spell (he claims) are discernible: lingering, travelling and loving. Death may be caused by the first, restlessness by the second (causing one to move from place to place) and devotion by the third. Certain perfumes are used in the latter case. Bitter apple root (he says) is an aid in such hexing.

A human skull is standard equipment in voodoo operations. Bones and stones are also used.

Voodoo carries with it the power of suggestion and is therefore widely successful. See hex.

voyage:
See journey; travelling.

W

Wagner, Richard:
See thirteen.

waiters at tables:
Drawing out a chair for a customer to be seated is a rite that is considered by many waiters bearing on a good tip. If a customer takes a seat other than that assigned this is a bad omen (small or no tip).

The fork must be near the plate and the knife on the outside and parallel. Any other arrangement forebodes bad luck.

It is auspicious to open the napkin for a customer. So also: to bring a second portion of butter before it is requested. If a customer, for any reason, sends out a dish this is an omen of bad luck for the remaining portion of the day.

Receiving a big tip early in the day is a bad omen. The rest will be meager. Breaking a dish is a bad omen (loss of position, small tips, etc.).

A waiter who is aware that a certain salutation is followed by a generous tip must employ the identical salutation on subsequent customers to insure good luck.

A customer who is a hunchback will bring good luck in the matter of tips. A one-armed customer forebodes bad luck.

walking:
Never allow anyone to pass between you and your companion while walking together. This brings bad luck. Should this happen, retrace your steps to the point of separation if you wish to counteract the spell. Or, say the words "bread and butter." Never pass an object (e.g., a pole) if it separates you and your companion. Both walk together around it. See athletes; "bread and butter"; rain; shoes; sleep walking; stepping on a crack.

238

walking backwards:
   See children.

walking under a ladder:
   A common omen of bad luck. A ladder placed in front of the Duluth Herald and News Tribune building to test the prevalence of this superstition showed recently that only five people out of more than twenty five walked under it in spite of the fact that it took more steps to walk around it (and without impediments in the way). Not all who did so would admit the superstition.

   If the ladder hangs horizontally there is no sign of either good or bad luck.

   It may be noted that this superstition is found among ancient Egyptians who held the belief that walking under a ladder involved the frightening experience of meeting a god going up or coming down. See ladders.

walks:
   See stepping on a crack.

wall paper:
   See birds.

walnut leaves:
   See fleas.

walnuts:
   See weather prognostication.

wand, magic:
   Every magician is supposed to have his wand. Fairies have always carried their long tapering wands. Kings wave their sceptres, symbols of authority, power and blessing. The rod and the staff of royalty are potent wands. North American Indians reserved the use of sceptres or wands for their chief and medicine men. The wand is a power; it controls Nature and bends the will of men.

239

wanderer:
  See teeth.

want:
  See fortune telling.

war, sign of an approaching:
  See harvest flies; shooting stars and comets.

warding off illness:
  See illness.

warm heart:
  See cold hands.

warning of death:
  It is held by some that death without warning never occurs. Among seafaring people the belief has been widely current that a sick person will not pass away until the tide ebbs.

wart:
  See mole or wart.

washing:
  Wash and wipe together
  Live and fight together (Maine).

washing blankets:
  See blankets.

washing clothes:
  "If you get wet when doing a laundry you will marry a drunkard."

washing dishes:
  See sleepy.

washing hair:
  If a lady washes her hair in water from March snow, it will become pretty. See baldness.

washing hands:
See friends; mole or wart.

wasp:
The wasp called the "velvet ant" or "cow ant" is supposed to be especially dangerous to livestock (although it is non-poisonous). The superstition in the south (U.S.A.) is that it is a "cow killer" (so called).

A wasp which flies into a house will bring good luck.

water:
Water is supposed to be fattening (although it has no calories). See dreams; finding water; iron water; jar of water with an immersed knife; muddy water; onions; pine bark; rain; rain water; storm; well water.

water finder:
See dowser.

water fowl:
See weather prognostication.

water lily roots:
Water lily roots mixed with boiled potatoes will "eat out proud flesh" (Maine). See cures.

watermelon:
See cures.

water smeller:
See dowser.

water witcher:
See dowser; fruit trees, grafting.

waving farewell:
Waving to friends in farewell until they are out of sight is to invite a permanent farewell. It is better to turn one's back after saying good-bye.

wax image:
See pin.

weak-minded:
See idiots.

wealth:
See birds; birth mark; cutting finger nails; financial prosperity; four-leaf clover; hair; marriage; mole or wart; money; riches; shooting stars and comets; sneezing.

weaning of babies:
See Good Friday.

wearing apparel:
See clothes; Ezzard Charles; garments; shirts.

wearing opals:
See opals, wearing.

wearing shamrocks:
See shamrock.

weather:
See April showers; fairy faith; marriage; May; milk; moon, the new; sailors; storm; umbrella; wedding day; wind.

weather prognostication:
A long hard winter is foreshadowed by New Englanders if the skunks come in early from the woods and find retreat under the barns, if the coats of foxes are heavy, if the nuts fall generously from the walnut trees, if muskrats are busy in erecting their homes along the brooks in great numbers and of greater size.

A sure sign of rain: in the barnyard the hens are "curling up and picking."

Crows giving forth a peculiar and unusual cry herald the coming of rain.

Dandelions blowing out full early in the day herald good weather.

If fish are biting eagerly and sport near the surface this heralds bad weather. (*The (Old) Farmer's Almanack* [1857])

A sky that is very red foretells wind or rain; but if the morning is gray, very red foretells a fine day.

An evening red and a morning gray
Will set the traveller on his way;
But an evening gray and a morning red
Will pour down rain on the pilgrim's head.
(New England)

If on the horizon a greenish color appears this is taken to be the sign of continued wet weather. In the autumn, the purple of the falling haze is the sign of good weather continuing. (New England)

If a section of blue sky appears on a rainy morning big enough "to make a Dutchman a pair of breeches" this is a sign of a fine afternoon (New England). (*The (Old) Farmer's Almanack* [1855].)

If butterflies appear early they are regarded (in New England lore) as bearers of the tidings of good weather.

If chickens are unusually noisy this is a sign of rain (New England).

If chickweed is open in the morning this is a sign of fair weather; if closed, rain. If it continues to unfold it is a good day; if the flowers withdraw, bad weather is ahead. Chickweed has been called the poor man's weatherglass.

Cobwebs on the grass early in the morning prophesy good weather.

A hard winter is ahead if the corn husks are difficult to pull apart. (*The (Old) Farmer's Almanack* [1856])

If moles cast up their hills this is a sign of rain; if horses stretch their necks, sniff the air, gather in the corner of the field, these are signs of rain; if rats or mice become restless and squeak, if dogs become sleepy and lethargic and eat grass, if cats lick their bodies and wash their faces, these are signs of showers.

If cattle cease their feeding and chase each other, if sheep spring about unusually in the pasture, these are signs of a change of the weather.

Unusual activity of ants, likewise, is a sign of rain. Before a storm they appear in great activity carrying their eggs from place to place. If before eleven in the morning the ants clear their holes and pile the dirt high, this is a sign of fair weather. (The above are New England superstitions.) "Stepping on an ant brings rain" is a common belief.

In New England animal behavior betokened weather changes.

Bats flitting about late in the evening foretell a fine spring or autumn day for the morrow. Bees remaining in their hives or flying only short distances foretell rain. Beetles flying about late at evening foreshadow a fine day for the morrow.

A gull flying inland reveals a brewing storm; flying toward the open sea, the return of fair weather. If swallows fly low this is the sign of storm approaching; if they fly high fair weather is ahead. If the blue jay approaches the house screaming it is a sign of bad weather. If the peacock squalls, if the guinea hen calls "come back," if the cock crows less than usual upon the fence, if the quail calls "more wet" noisily, bad weather is approaching. Other signs of storms: cawing of the crow, screeching of the owl and water fowl, loud singing of the thrush, birds picking their feathers and flying to their nests.

When gulls are seen flying high over the harbor it is a sign (in Provincetown harbor) of bad weather ahead.

When oysters bed deep (Well-fleet) it is a sign of a hard winter and Provincetown harbor will fill with ice pack in February.

If a chicken's gizzard comes out easily from the inner skin this is a sign of an "open water."

If asses bray unusually and shake their ears, this is a sign of rain:

244

When the ass begins to bray
We surely shall have rain that day.

When the donkey blows his horn
'Tis time to house your hay and corn.

If swine become restless, if they grunt loudly, jerk their heads, this is a sign of high winds.

Wind or rain is approaching if gnats bite more and if they fly near the ground or assemble under trees. If they move about gingerly in the open air at evening it is a sign of heat. Rain is approaching if hawkweed open their flowers at morning or close them in the afternoon. (*The (Old) Farmer's Almanack* [1859])

The clamorous croaking of frogs is a sign of rain. So also the restlessness of congregating toads.

The migration southward or westward of geese in greater numbers in autumn indicates a hard winter ahead; to the north, a siege of hot weather. (*The (Old) Farmer's Almanack* [1858])

Rainbow in the morning;
Sailors take warning.
Rainbow at night
Sailors delight.
Rainbow at noon
Rain very soon (New England).

Among Southern mountaineers it is a sign of fair weather if a cat washes itself in a usual manner; however, if it licks the fur in an unusual manner or sits with its tail toward the fire or washes above its ears, this is a sign of a weather change.

Rain before seven
Clear before 'leven. (New England)

Sun at seven
Rain at 'leven. (New England)

Insects, particularly flies, if more obnoxious than usual by
their bites and stings are indicating a siege of rainy weather.
(New England) Particularly is this true of horse flies.

Flowers, observed Linnaeus, the Swedish botanist, are certain indicators of weather changes.

The doggerel concerning the onion is familiar among
farmers:

Onion's skin very thin
Mild winter coming in.
Onion's skin thick and tough
Coming winter cold and rough.

Bees figure in weather prognostication:

When bees to distance wing their flight
Days are warm and skies are bright.
But when the flight ends near their home
Stormy weather is sure to come.

A forecast of severe winter ahead (in Maine) is seen
when large stores of honey are laid up by bees.

From Maine lore:

"Sun sets Friday clear as bell
Rain on Monday sure as hell."

"Colder the night
When the stars shine bright."

"Just so far as the sun shines in
Just so far will the snow blow in." (Feb. 2)

246

"Mackerel skies and mares' tails
Make tall ships carry low sails."

"Between the hours of ten and two
Will show you what the weather will do."

"Rain on the flood, only a scud
Rain on the ebb, sailors to bed."

"An easterly glin
Sure sign of a wet skin."

"Wild geese, wild geese, gangin' out to sea
All good weather it will be."

"Rooster crowing on the fence
Rain will go hence.
Rooster crowing on the ground
Rain surely will come down."

"If a rooster crows before going to bed
He will rise with a wet head."

See birds; Candlemas Day; car washing; Christmas prognostication; crickets; Easter Sunday; fishing; ground hog; harvest flies; katydid; March; moon; rabbit; rain; rake; storm; thunder; Wednesday; wind, the.

weaving:
See fairy faith.

wedding:
See bride; bridegroom; bridesmaid; dreams; groom; marriage; rice throwing; sewing; shoes.

wedding anniversaries:
Milestones along the course of life have been celebrated over many centuries. Particularly has this been so with wedding anniversaries. Certain gifts became associated with cer-

tain anniversaries in the belief of their peculiar propriety and symbol of good luck. Gems and precious stones became associated as special tokens for certain years. These tokens have become more or less standardized (not only gems and stones but other materials as well).

The following list shows the prevailing token for the anniversary year:

1st anniversary—paper
2nd—cotton
3rd—linen
4th—book
5th—wood
6th—iron
7th—copper, bronze
8th—leather
9th—pottery
10th—tin, aluminum
12th—silk, linen
13th—moonstone
14th—moss-agate
15th—rock-crystal or glass
16th—topaz or topaz-quartz
17th—amethyst
18th—garnet
19th—hyacinth
20th—china
23rd—sapphire
25th—silver
26th—star sapphire, blue
30th—pearl
35th—coral
39th—cat's eye
40th—ruby
45th—Alexandrite
50th—gold

52nd—star-ruby
55th—emerald
60th—diamond, yellow
65th—star-sapphire, gray
67th—star-sapphire, purple
75th—diamond.

Substitute gems for the number 13 and its multiples (regarded as unlucky) are selected which possess the feature of
moving light to offset the influence of bad luck (e.g., numbers 13, 26, 39).

wedding, approaching:

See bride; butterfly; falling upstairs; groom; hand shaking;
jumping out of bed; marriage prospects; peeling of an apple;
rhyme making; sewing; sneezing; table sitting.

wedding cake:

Under a girl's pillow a piece of wedding cake will serve to
bring on a dream of her future husband. If she dreams three
nights in succession whatever dream occurs the third night
will come true (New England).

wedding dates:

See marriage.

wedding day:

It is an omen of a stormy married life if the day of the
wedding turns out to be stormy. On the contrary, a pleasant
married life is forecast if the wedding day is pleasant (New
England). See marriage.

wedding ring:

Rubbed three times on the eye a wedding ring will cure a
stye.

Turned around three times it will help make a wish come
true.

It is unlucky to remove a wedding ring except in an
emergency.

A broken wedding ring is a sign of marital difficulties. When worn thin it brings luck to the wearer's children.

A plain gold wedding ring is a remedy for sore eyes. See circle; fortune telling.

Wednesday:

The sun always shines on Wednesday because God created the sun on Wednesday. See cutting finger nails; days of the week; fortune telling; moving into a new home; sneezing.

weed, white:

See petals, white weed.

week days:

See days of the week; under separate headings of days.

Weemans, the:

See rappings.

well water:

An old belief maintains that one will grow tall if one drinks well water.

west wind:

See wind.

whiskey:

See colds.

whistling:

A whistling girl and a crowing hen
Always come to no good end.

If little girls whistle they will grow a beard.

Whistling incites courage and is particularly helpful in the night when you follow a lonely path.

Whistling in a house is to invite bad luck.

Whistling aboard ship brings bad luck. This superstition

is still of vital consideration among sailors. (It has been said by one who has spent his life aboard ships that if anyone persists in whistling on board he is apt to suffer a black eye at the hands of his fellow sailors.) This superstition may have come about for a good practical reason: a whistle sounds much the same as a bosun pipe (of useful purpose) and confusion resulted. In a sailing ship a whistle is said to bring on a wind (unfavorable to its course). See sailors; theatre.

whistling back stage:
Among actors whistling back stage is unlucky.

white:
This is the color of innocence. Thus, brides dress in white. See colors; sewing.

white foot horse:
See horse buying.

white hair:
See hair.

white horse:
See dreams; horse; horsemen; red head girls.

white man:
See racial superstition.

white marks on finger nails:
See fortune telling.

white people:
See sunstroke.

white weed petals:
See petals, white weed.

white wine:
See cures; moon.

whooping cough:
If a live fuzzy caterpillar is sewed into a cloth sack and

251

hung by a cord around the neck—this will alleviate the horrible illness of whooping cough. This superstition persisted until quite recently.

widow:
See sewing.

widow's peak:
See hair line.

wigs:
See theatre.

wild cat grease:
See cures.

will power:
See chin and jaw.

Wilson, Woodrow:
See thirteen.

wind, the:

Wind from the east—bad for man and for beast;
Wind from the south is too hot for them both;
Wind from the north is of very little worth;
Wind from the west is the softest and the best.
(The (Old) Farmer's Almanack [1851])

When the wind is in the east
Then the sap will run the least.
When the wind is in the west
Then the sap will run the best. (New England)

See fishing; storm; weather prognostication.

winding a piece of cotton:
See theatre.

wine:

See white wine.

wine passing:

Passing wine at the table with the right hand gives good luck. See toasting.

winter:

See rabbit; weather prognostication.

wiping:

See washing.

wiping on a towel:

Do not wipe at the same time on the same towel with another person; otherwise there will be a quarrel between you and the other one (New England).

wisdom:

See colors; crust and crumbs; lucky; palmistry.

wish bone:

See birds; chicken's wishbone.

wish come true:

If the drop of juice which is pressed by the thumb nail to the top of one grass stalk "took off" the drop from the stalk held against it, the wish would come true. (New England) See birds; blowing out birthday candles; star falling; star, first.

wishing:

See chicken's wishbone; crossing the fingers; lady bug; moon, the new; robin; shooting stars and comets; wedding ring.

wit:

See palmistry.

witches:

Persons believed to have access to the will of the devil and to carry out his decree are witches. Believed to be endowed with infernal power, to foretell events, to destroy, to afflict, they are sort of devil ambassadors.

Witches' Sabbaths or meetings were supposed to be held four times a year: Candlemas (February 2), Roodmas (April 30), Lammas (August 1) and Hallowe'en (October 31). To these meetings witches rode on broomsticks, rakes, goats, dogs or pokers. Satan (in the form of a goat) was master of ceremonies. Before him witches appeared naked but smeared with ointment of unbaptized infants.

Biblical injunction against these horrible creatures: "Thou shalt not suffer a witch to live." (Ex. 22:18)

In Massachusetts in 1641 witchcraft became a capital offense and in 1642 in Connecticut. The case of Alse Young of Windsor, Connecticut, a witch, involved a trial, pronouncement of guilt and execution. In 1648 Margaret Jones, Boston, was hanged (she claimed healing powers with certain herbs). Ann Hibbins, a widow of a Boston merchant, was hanged.

The most famous case of American witch hunting occurred in Salem, Massachusetts (Danvers) in the winter of 1691-1692. In the home of the Rev. Samuel Parris there began a series of meetings in 1691 to study fortune telling, magic, etc. This group was made up of three married women, a slave (named Tibuta) and ten girls (ages nine to twenty). As the winter wore on the girls were known in the community to act queerly. They barked like dogs, screamed at unseen objects and went into spasms or fits. The village physician upon examination announced that the girls were indulging in witchcraft. The girls in turn pointed their fingers at Tibuta as the witch. The slave girl after being tortured confessed and was hanged. Then their fingers pointed at Sarah Good and Sarah Osburn. These two were then hanged. Later the girls pointed to others whom they disliked, e.g., the whole John Proctor family, Doreas Good, the Rev. Samuel Willard, minister of Old South Church (Boston), and John Alden. Their fingers pointed at Mrs. Hale, minister's wife of Beverly. Mrs. Hale had too good a reputation to be tarnished by such accusations. Forthwith the governor of Massachusetts ordered the release of all those who had been imprisoned because of "witchcraft." The Salem incident brought on nineteen deaths by hanging, two deaths by imprisonment and physical and mental torture to many. The Salem incident was only a chapter of a series of similar events going on at the time in Europe in which respectable church people including the clergy suffered charges of witchcraft practicing by fellow townsmen. Scottish Presbyterians in 1773 affirmed their belief in witchcraft as did John Wesley, Cotton Mather and many other well known leaders.

In 1936 (October 2nd) in Woodbridge, New Jersey, witchcraft was revived in full stature. Three women testified in court that a neighbor woman (Mrs. Czinkota) was a witch, having the power of changing her figure, making up mysterious brews and engaging in fantastic rituals. "I saw her head shrink to the size of my fist" said one. "Horns appeared on her head and she would walk on all fours like an animal. . . . She changed herself into a horse. I saw her head down and change into a dog." Some members of the community took precautions to guard themselves as the horror-tales circulated.

A witch among humans is to be recognized as having eyebrows that meet over the nose, some birthmark, eyes that peer deeply and even red hair.

The existence of witches was widely accepted by people of all classes. In 1736 British law moved in against this belief by depriving witches of legal standing.

A piece of iron placed under a door will keep witches away. See birds; egg shells; fairy faith; hex; horse(s); sailors; water witches.

wolf dog:
See cures.

wolf's teeth:
See cures.

women:
See corner stone laying; marriage prospects; mole or wart; moon; name changing; New Year; preachers and women; red head girls; starting on a journey; whistling; witches.

wonder:
See phrenology.

wood:
See knock on wood; touch wood; wedding anniversaries.

woolen sock:
See colds.

words:
Words act as charms. For success in hunting, a muttering of a number of meaningless formulae in a low voice is said to bring good luck (Eskimos). Words repeated nine times (sometimes with the sign of the cross) with a finger over an injury will charm away the ills of burns, canker sores, etc.

The abracadabra (written out in full at the top, the next lower line indented with the final letter omitted and succeeding lower lines similarly indented with last letter omitted forms a triangle) spelled out on paper, folded in the form of a cross and worn as an amulet for nine days, then thrown backwards before sunrise into a stream flowing eastward—brings good luck and cures ills. (This ancient practice has persisted for centuries, claiming remarkable success.)

Words may not be uttered but concentrated upon and, with the use of the mouth on a sore, will perform the function of healing. See boasting; churning; cledonism; preaching to the fish.

words, magical:
See bees; cleromancy; Gesundheit; magical words.

work:
See fortune telling.

"worms":
See grinding of teeth; pumpkins.

wrong side:
See getting out of bed.

wrong side dressing:
See clothing, putting on.

Y

yawning:

An ancient superstition holds that a yawn makes possible the entrance of the devil into the mouth; hence, one must hold a hand over the mouth to protect oneself. It is considered a bad portent to yawn during prayers. See evil eye.

yellow:

A most unlucky color to many actors is yellow. Fay Bainter has remarked about being warned at wearing yellow. Managers of road shows have been known to inspect troupe baggage to make certain no yellow trunks were included or even yellow stickers on baggage. See athletes; colors; diamond, yellow; dog.

yellow curtain:

See theatre.

yellow dog:

See dog.

young:

See theatre.

young people:

Young people should not sleep with elderly people because the latter will draw vitality from the former and thus weaken them. Only the elders benefit in such bed partnerships (New England). See sleep; sleeping.

youth:

See fountain of youth.

Yule log:

See Christmas.

Z

Zadkiel's Almanac:
See magic crystal.

Ziegfeld, F.:
See thirteen.

Zodiac, the:
See astrology; birth stones; moon; potatoes, planting.